POLICE
IN AMERICA

THE BOSTON POLICE STRIKE

Two Reports

ARNO PRESS & THE NEW YORK TIMES
NEW YORK,   1971

Reprint Edition 1971 by Arno Press Inc.

Reprinted from copies in
The University of Illinois Library

LC# 75-154572
ISBN 0-405-03362-1

Police In America
ISBN for complete set: 0-405-03360-5
See last pages of this volume for titles.

Manufactured in the United States of America

CONTENTS

FOURTEENTH ANNUAL REPORT

OF THE

POLICE COMMISSIONER

FOR THE

CITY OF BOSTON

YEAR ENDING NOVEMBER 30, 1919

BOSTON
WRIGHT & POTTER PRINTING CO., STATE PRINTERS
32 DERNE STREET
1920

CONTENTS.

The Commonwealth of Massachusetts.

REPORT.

HEADQUARTERS OF THE POLICE DEPARTMENT,
OFFICE OF THE POLICE COMMISSIONER, 29 PEMBERTON SQUARE,
BOSTON, Nov. 30, 1919.

To His Excellency CALVIN COOLIDGE, *Governor.*

YOUR EXCELLENCY: — As Police Commissioner for the City of Boston I have the honor to present, in compliance with the provisions of chapter 291 of the Acts of 1906, a report of the police department for the year ending Nov. 30, 1919.

Having been appointed Police Commissioner by Governor Samuel W. McCall, I assumed the office on Dec. 30, 1918, succeeding the late Stephen O'Meara. This report, the first that I have the honor to make, must of necessity deal principally with the greatest crisis the police department of Boston has ever passed through, — namely, the so-called strike of the police. This occurrence was so unprecedented in this country, so antagonistic to the fundamentals of government, and had such a revolutionary effect upon the police department itself that it seems fitting that the circumstances should be reviewed in considerable detail.

ABANDONMENT OF DUTY BY THE POLICE FORCE.

At 5.45 P.M. Tuesday, Sept. 9, 1919, 1,117 patrolmen out of 1,544 in the department abandoned their office as police, or, as it is more commonly termed, "struck." The sole issue involved in the "strike," — and the issue never changed, notwithstanding there was much public discussion of other questions not involved, — was whether the Boston police force as a body should be allowed to affiliate with the American Federation of Labor. The matter of improvement of the conditions of the station houses was not an issue, for the men thoroughly understood that the Commissioner had taken all steps possible to relieve these conditions. Chapter 291, Acts of 1906, provides that "the city of Boston shall provide all such accommodations for the police of said city as said police commissioner may require." Within ten weeks of my assuming office I appointed a committee, consisting of a captain, lieutenant and sergeant, to examine every station house in this department, and report to me fully in regard to each station. The committee performed its duties and gave me a detailed report on the condition of every station house in the city of Boston, the city prison and the house of detention. On April 10, I forwarded to his honor the mayor a copy of said report, together with my recommendations and suggestions. His honor is, no doubt, proceeding with all the expedition possible, to obtain the necessary appropriations. This the patrolmen knew.

The question of wages was not an issue, because wages of patrolmen are fixed by concurrent action of the mayor and the Police Commissioner. The Police Commissioner is responsible for the $200 increase in salaries that was given this year, and which was all the men asked for, and it was understood that that increase was not final, but that no further increases would be made until the superior officers, whose salaries have not been increased, were also taken care of. The absurdity of giving the patrolmen more than a sergeant is perfectly apparent. This the men understood.

Inability to obtain a hearing on grievances or obtain access to the Commissioner was not an issue, because the Police Commissioner had established an additional avenue by which the men could reach him independent of their superior officers. At the suggestion of the Commissioner a delegate from each station was elected for the purpose by ballot by the men themselves. These delegates met, organized and appointed a grievance committee. How well that worked is shown by the following copy of a letter from the grievance committee, dated as late as July 16: —

BOSTON, MASS., July 16, 1919.

Hon. EDWIN U. CURTIS, *Police Commissioner, Boston, Mass.*

DEAR SIR: — We take this opportunity to thank you sincerely in behalf of all the patrolmen of the Boston police department for the many vital and important benefits obtained and which were championed by you, including the non-contributory pension, corrections in the rule relating to the unnecessary reporting by night men on their off days, and excuses from different roll calls. We desire to express our deep sense of gratitude for your efforts in our behalf in obtaining the increase in salary.

With assurance of our highest considerations and esteem, we remain,

Very respectfully,

GRIEVANCE COMMITTEE,
MICHAEL LYNCH,
President.
JOHN J. HARNEY,
Secretary.

That the men had no grievance or quarrel with the Commissioner, and their relations were apparently very friendly, appears from a letter of the Boston Social Club, as follows: —

BOSTON SOCIAL CLUB, May 13, 1919.

E. U. CURTIS, *Police Commissioner for the City of Boston.*

DEAR SIR: — At a meeting of the Boston Social Club, held at International Hall, 67 Warren Street, Roxbury, Friday evening, May 9, by unanimous vote, a vote of thanks is hereby extended to you for your kind consideration in furnishing at your personal expense refreshments to the police officers detailed for duty at the parade of the 26th Division of the American Expeditionary Forces on April 25 last past.

This kindness, as well as many others for their welfare put into active operation by you since assuming your important office, is highly appreciated by the patrolmen of the police department, for which we sincerely thank you.

Yours very respectfully,

JOSEPH J. McGILLIVRAY,
Secretary.

As has been stated, the sole issue in this matter was and is whether the Boston police force as a body should be allowed to affiliate with the American Federation of Labor. The only possible ground a Police Commissioner, duly appointed and responsible to the Commonwealth and bound by his oath of office, could take forbade his recognizing any divided allegiance in the police force. It was clearly pointed out by the entire press of Boston, with the exception of one paper, that there should be no unionization of the police force. The one newspaper that did not at that time condemn editorially the project did not support it. Its editorial columns were silent. Moreover, the project received the express condemnation of my predecessor in office, Mr. O'Meara, and there are herewith submitted extracts from a General Order on the subject, which he issued under date of June 28, 1918.

It is probable that the printed rumors to the effect that members of the police department are discussing the advisability of organizing a union to be affiliated with the American Federation of Labor represent no substantial sentiment existing among them. Under ordinary conditions no attention would be paid to such rumors, but even though unfounded they are so likely to injure the discipline, efficiency and even the good name of the force, and the times are so favorable to the creation of discontent among men who are bearing their share of the war burdens, though still at home, that I feel it to be my duty to make the situation clear.

There is no substantial disagreement as to the wisdom and even the necessity of maintaining unions among persons following the same industrial occupations.

Though a union of public employees, as distinct from those composed of employees of private concerns, is in itself a matter of doubtful propriety, such union in any case and at the worst could affect the operations only of a particular branch of the city service. The police department, on the other hand, exists for the impartial enforcement of the laws and the protection of persons and property under all conditions. Should its members incur obligations to an outside organization, they would be justly suspected of abandoning the impartial attitude which heretofore has vindicated their good faith as against the complaints almost invariably made by both sides in many controversies.

It is assumed erroneously that agents of an outside organization could obtain for the police advantages in pay and regulations. This is not a question of compelling a private employer to surrender a part of his profits; it has to do with police service, which is wholly different from any other service, public or private, — a service regulated by laws which hold to a strict responsibility certain officials, of whom the Police Commissioner is one. The policemen are their own best advocates, and to suppose that an official would yield on points of pay or regulation to the arguments or threats of an outside organization if the policemen themselves had failed to establish their case would be to mark him as cowardly and unfit for his position.

I cannot believe that a proposition to turn the police force into a union, subject to the rules and direction of any organization outside the police department, will ever be presented formally to its members, but if, unfortunately, such a question should ever arise, I trust that it will be answered with an emphatic refusal by the members of the force who have an intelligent regard for their own self-respect, the credit of the department, and the obligations to the whole public which they undertook with their oath of office.

In the early spring rumors again began to arise that the movement to unionize the force, which apparently had been stopped by Mr. O'Meara's clear disapproval, was starting up again. I am informed that the matter was brought before the men's organization, and the proposal defeated. It was then reported that papers were being circulated for signatures in every station house, making application for a charter in the American Federation of Labor. A statement was at once issued to the press by the Commissioner disapproving the movement. It soon became apparent, however, that the men back of the movement were disregarding the Commissioner's views thus made public. It became necessary, therefore, to issue a General Order on the subject, which was done on July 29, 1919, in the following words: —

I note that a movement among the members of the Boston police force to affiliate with the American Federation of Labor is actively on foot. I had hoped that the older men in the service who have served under my predecessor, Stephen O'Meara, who understood his attitude on such matters would have speedily and effectually terminated such a movement. Mr. O'Meara issued a General Order to the police force on June 28, 1918. I repeat to the members of the force what he said in that General Order, and trust that every member of the force will weigh every word carefully.

The portion of Mr. O'Meara's order appearing in the first part of this report was then quoted, and the order was concluded as follows: —

I desire to say to the members of the force that I am firmly of the opinion that a police officer cannot consistently belong to a union and perform his sworn duty. I am not an opponent of labor unions, and neither was Mr. O'Meara. He pointed out in well-chosen language that there is no question in the police department as to how much of an employer's profits should be shared with the workers. Policemen are public officers. They have taken an oath of office. That oath requires them to carry out the law with strict impartiality, no matter what their personal feeling may be. The laws they carry out are laws made by the representatives of the people assembled in the Legislature. Therefore it should be apparent that the men to whom the carrying out of these laws is entrusted should not be subject to the orders or the dictation of any organization, no matter what, that comprises only one part of the general public. A man who enters the police force, as I have stated, takes an oath of office, and he should realize that his work is sharply differentiated from that of the worker in private employ. It is difficult to see, under these circumstances, what a policeman can hope to gain by the proposed affiliation, although it is easy to see how the other affiliated bodies may gain a great deal. Mr. O'Meara put it well when he said that "the policemen are their own best advocates, and to suppose that an official would yield on points of pay or regulation to the arguments or threats of an outside organization if the policemen themselves had failed to establish their case would be to mark him as cowardly and unfit for his position."

As Police Commissioner for the City of Boston I feel it my duty to say to the police force that I disapprove of the movement on foot; that in my opinion it is not for the best interests of the men themselves; and that beyond question it is not for the best interest of the general public, which this department is required to serve.

When it became evident that no attention was paid to the disapproval of both the present and former Commissioner, I was compelled to promulgate the rule, which with its preamble is herewith set forth: —

BOSTON, Aug. 11, 1919.

GENERAL ORDER No. 110.

It is or should be apparent to any thinking person that the police department of this or any other city cannot fulfil its duty to the entire public if its members are subject to the direction of an organization existing outside the department._ It is a well-recognized fact that a police officer is not an employee but a State officer. He is charged with an impartial enforcement of the laws under the direction of a commissioner who is himself a statutory officer. The following rule interferes in no wise in a policeman's interests and activities as a man and a citizen. It does, however, forbid him and the department from coming under the direction and dictation of any organization which represents but one element or class of the community. If troubles and disturbances arise where the interests of this organization and the interests of other elements and classes in the community conflict, the situation immediately arises that always arises when a man attempts to serve two masters, — he must fail either in his duty as a policeman, or in his obligation to the organization that controls him. Therefore the following is hereby added to and made a part of Rule 35 of the Rules and Regulations, and designated as section 19 of said rule: —

19. No member of the force shall join or belong to any organization, club or body composed of present or present and past members of the force which is affiliated with or a part of any organization, club or body outside the department, except that a post of the Grand Army of the Republic, the United Spanish War Veterans and the American Legion of World's War Veterans may be formed within the department.

No attention was paid to the rule; it was deliberately disregarded. The men met, organized and elected officers August 15.

The men reported to have been elected officers were questioned as to their connection with the organization, and charges of having violated the rule were then brought against them.

Eight men were placed on trial August 26; eleven men on August 29.

By request of counsel for the men the Police Commissioner heard the cases himself.

There was no denial of the facts. Counsel for the defendants argued that the rule was invalid, unreasonable and contrary to the express law of Massachusetts.

Counsel quoted in support of the men's position a Massachusetts statute, Acts of 1909, chapter 514, section 19, but neglected to state, which is the fact, that a like statute had been declared unconstitutional by the Supreme Court of the United States in Coppage v. Kansas, 236 U. S. 1.

Counsel also quoted an Illinois decision of a lower court which decided that the school board could not pass a rule forbidding school teachers to join a union and refusing to employ those who did so (Appl. CD. Ill. 199 Ill. Appl. 356), but also neglected to state that this was a lower court decision which had been overruled by the Supreme Court of Illinois, and was not and never has been the law of Illinois. (See People *v.* City of Chicago, 278 Ill. 318.)

On September 4 the Police Commissioner was ready to hand down his decision, and notified the men's counsel to be at his office to receive the decision. While they were there, and before the decision had been announced, a letter arrived from his honor the mayor, asking a continuance of the Commissioner's finding. This request was communicated to the defendant's counsel, and the Commissioner stated to the counsel that the request was one which should properly come from them, and asked if they requested the continuance. They replied that they were indifferent, and refused to request the continuance themselves. They even refused to say that they assented to the continuance.

Although sitting in judgment in this case, and feeling that requests having to do with the case should come from the parties interested, the Commissioner continued his findings until September 8, counsel for the men having reluctantly agreed to say that they did not object to the continuance.

It must be observed that there was ample opportunity between August 11, the day the order against affiliation was promulgated, and September 8 for these men and the other patrolmen in the department to give up their affiliation with the American Federation of Labor had they. desired to do so. But it cannot be emphasized too strongly that at no time was it ever even intimated to the Commissioner that the men would abandon their union.

So much has been said about a certain plan proposed for a settlement of the trouble that the Commissioner's position should be made clear on this point. The plan, in substance, was this: —

1. That the policemen's union should not affiliate with any labor organization, but should retain its independence

and maintain its organization for the purpose of assisting its members concerning all questions relating to hours, pay and physical conditions.

2. That the present wages, hours and working conditions should be investigated by a committee of three citizens selected by the concurrent action of the mayor, the Commissioner and the policemen's union, and their conclusions communicated to the mayor, and that thereafter any differences which might arise between the Commissioner and the union relative to hours, wages and physical conditions of work which could not be adjusted should be submitted to three citizens of Boston, selected by agreement between the Police Commissioner, the mayor and the policemen's union, and that the conclusions of this committee should be submitted to the mayor, the Police Commissioner and the citizens of Boston.

3. That nothing should be done to discourage any members of the Boston police force from becoming or continuing to be members of the policemen's union, and that no discrimination should be made on account of such membership.

4. That there should be no discrimination on the part of the members of the policemen's union, or any of them, against a police officer who refused to join the union.

5. That no member of the union should be discriminated against because of any previous affiliation with the American Federation of Labor.

In the first place, this plan was merely brought to the attention of the Commissioner and was not prepared by the men, and the attitude of the men in regard to it was in no way indicated. It must be borne in mind that at the time this plan was presented I was sitting in judgment on the cases of nineteen men charged with violating the rule. While the attitude of these men as to future violation of the rule was of importance, it was of importance only, in the event of their being found guilty, in mitigation of the sentence to be imposed. So far as the men on trial were concerned, the plan gave no evidence whatever of any change of heart or attitude, and if such had been its object, it should have been urged by the men themselves, or their counsel speaking for them. I have never been able to understand why any one who approved the rule and condemned the violation of it could have expected me to dicker with its violators, or that I, rather than they, should make the offer of compromise. The suggestion would have been impossible enough, even if the men or their counsel had asked me to agree to drop the proceedings and put the plan into operation on the agreement of the union to surrender its charter.

So far as the plan itself was concerned, if it was not intended as a basis of compromise of the cases on trial it had no connection with these cases, and its merits could properly come up for discussion only after the men on trial had purged themselves of their violation of a rule of the department. As to the arbitration features of the plan, it should be said that nowhere in the statute by virtue of which the Police Commissioner holds office is there any language that authorizes or permits him to divide his authority and responsibility with any one. The proposal that he should do so is both novel and fundamentally incompatible with the responsibility to the public which the law casts upon the Commissioner for the government of a police force, and with the sense of responsibility to the Commissioner which the members of the force must feel if proper discipline and efficiency are to be maintained. The plan was a reversion to the state of divided responsibility, vacillating policy and dilatory action, which prompted the Legislature to first take the control of the police force of Boston from three commissioners appointed by and subservient to the mayors of Boston, and to place that control in a board of three appointed by the Governor; and then, later, to still further concentrate responsibility by transferring the control to a single commissioner, under the present law.

The Commissioner rendered his decision on the nineteen men on trial on September 8. They were found guilty and were suspended. It should be especially noted that they were suspended and not discharged, because if they had been discharged they could not have been thereafter reinstated on the force. An opportunity to retract, if they had the inclination, was still left open to them and the other members of the force. This opportunity was flouted; the men persisted in their course; a secret ballot was taken; and, in pursuance of the vote, the majority of the patrolmen abandoned their office, when and with what results now so well known.

As criticism has been made because the State Guard was not in readiness to patrol the streets the evening and night of the desertion of the police, it may not be inadvisable to call attention to facts which apparently are not generally known.

The maintenance of law and order under ordinary conditions is imposed by law almost exclusively upon the authorities and police departments of the cities and towns of the Commonwealth. A few years ago a bill was reported to the Legislature by a commission appointed to study the question, which, if it had passed, would have provided a form of police reserve throughout the State capable of being assembled and held in readiness at points where conditions such as those in Boston existed. This bill, however, did not become law, so that each community was left for protection, as before, to its own resources in its own police department, or to such citizens as might temporarily be invested with police power. It is only when "tumult, riot or mob is threatened, or in case of public catastrophe when the usual police provisions are inadequate to preserve order and afford protection to persons and property," that St. 1917, chapter 327, section 26, allows the mayor of a city for his community, or the Governor of the Commonwealth for the State, to call upon the State Guard to aid the civil authorities. No authority at all is given the Commissioner himself, nor can the Governor or mayor invoke this aid merely because there is possibility of rioting. If it were otherwise it would make the State Guard subject to be called by the mayor of a city on every occasion when a more than usual crowd was collected, or when, for the moment, the resources of the local police force seemed overtaxed. As the court has said in regard to this law in an earlier form, it does not even enlarge the power of the civil officers by giving them any military authority, but only places at their disposal, in the exercise of their appropriate and legal functions, an organized and equipped body of men "capable of more efficient action in an emergency, and among a multitude, than an ordinary police force." (Ela v. Smith et als., 5 Gray, 121.) To invoke this statute the mayor or the Governor must at least have reasonable grounds for the belief, not only that rioting actually threatens, but that the usual provisions for policing are inadequate.

At 5.45 P.M. September 9, when the policemen of Boston deserted, neither of the conditions under which the law authorizes the calling of the State Guard existed. The streets of Boston were quiet, there were no threats of rioting or disorder, and no part of the population, except, perhaps, the policemen themselves, were in that state of excitement or stirred by those passions which are the precursors of rioting. Furthermore, up to the very moment the policemen deserted, the "usual police provisions" which the statute refers to could not be called inadequate, because until that moment the Boston police department was at full strength and per- forming its full duty. Not only this, but up to that moment there was no certainty, even, that the police force of Boston would actually desert that duty. Most diligent inquiries had been made throughout the department by the superior officers who, through personal contact with the men at the stations, many of whom they had known for years, were in the best position to size up the situation. Yet this most careful canvass did not produce any definite information either in respect to the number of members of the union, or whether a strike had been determined upon, or, if so, when it would probably take place, or how many of the men, if any, would desert. It was known with certainty that many of the men would remain loyal in any event. Such information as the Commissioner and others had been able to obtain in this and other ways tended to show that, in case a strike was called, 700 or 800 patrolmen would refuse to desert. This number, reinforced by State and metropoli- tan park police, would have left a substantial force adequate to tide over the emergency. In a strike against a private concern the strikers generally name a date when they will walk out if their demands are not granted. In this "strike" against public safety, however, no such amenity was observed. The time fixed was suddenly and secretly determined upon. The Commissioner was given no notice. It was the obvious policy on the part of the deserters to conceal their intentions to the last moment. Their success depended upon deception, secrecy and surprise. The meetings of the union were in secret. The press could get no definite information, and every time it quoted an officer or member of the union as to what was done in the meetings, that officer or member was quoted as saying that the word "strike" had never been mentioned. This state of uncertainty had existed some days before September 9. These facts were known by the mayor and the Governor, and obviously were not sufficient to warrant them, under the law, in calling out the State Guard Tuesday, any more than on several of the preceding days. When disorder broke out the mayor was notified and then called on the State Guard. It is unfortunate that there were no provisions of law adequate to meet the circumstances of this extraordinary situation. But prior to the events of the evening of September 9 a suggestion that a law was needed creating a reserve of police officers who could be assigned anywhere at a moment's notice to take the place of striking police officers would have excited ridicule.

As the law did not permit holding the State Guard in readiness to take up the policing of Boston at a moment's notice at any time during the week or ten days of suspense immediately preceding the "strike," the Commissioner was left to the ordinary resources provided by the law. This consisted almost solely of authority to appoint special or temporary police who might be substituted for the regular police. The difficulties with which this limitation of authority hampered the Commissioner are apparent on slight reflection. It is not every man who is fitted to perform police duty, and few men who are so fitted can afford to give up their jobs or occupations to become special police for a short time, either with or without pay. The Commissioner was, therefore, compelled by force of circumstances to organize a reserve police force from those public-spirited men who were so situated as to be able to afford to volunteer to take up police duty at a moment's notice. Some time before the strike actually took place measures were taken to organize such a force.

Measures taken for the Protection of the City.

First. Volunteer Policemen. — Former high police officials headed by former Superintendent Pierce, on pension, were called to duty and put in charge of enrolling a volunteer police force. At the time of the abandonment of duty there was a substantial number of volunteer police. As the patrolmen who are now out carried on their purpose in secret, however, it was not possible to put these men in the station houses at once. Such a force, composed of men who had their ordinary duties to attend to, could not have been kept mobilized during the time that rumors of "strike" were in the air, nor would it have been expedient to put them in the station houses while the regular force remained. It can be readily seen that to put a volunteer police force into a station before the regular police officers had abandoned their positions would have given the regular men an opportunity to say that they were distrusted by the Commissioner. Moreover, the volunteer police officers could not be furnished with arms until they had been surrendered by the regular patrolmen.

Second. — For some time previous the police department was busy swearing in special policemen among the employees of business houses of Boston for the protection of property where they were employed. The Police Commissioner never had any power to call the State Guard, but had consulted with His Excellency, and by reason of such consultation the Adjutant-General prepared for the most prompt mobilization of the troops if the emergency should arise.

Third. — The Police Commissioner also arranged, through the Governor, for the largest possible number of the metropolitan park police force and of the State police force. That resulted in over 60 State police being on duty and 100 park police.

Subsequent events have shown that the metropolitan park police did not render the efficient service the Police Commissioner had the right to expect.

Fourth. — On September 8, the day before the policemen abandoned their duty, the commanding officers of the several police divisions, in conference with the Commissioner and superintendent, gave it as their best judgment that nearly 800 patrolmen would remain on duty. As a matter of fact, somewhat over 400 did remain on duty, and were on duty that night. Vacations and days off were suspended, and there were also in the police department 225 superior officers who remained on duty and who did police work.

Fifth. — Section 26 of chapter 327 of the Acts of 1917 justifies the calling out of the troops only when there is "a tumult, riot or mob, or body of persons acting together by force to violate or resist laws of the Commonwealth or when such tumult, riot or mob is threatened." No such conditions contemplated by the statute appeared until the night of the 9th or the morning of the 10th, when the Commissioner notified the mayor that in his judgment the troops should be called, and the mayor made the call. Subsequently His Excellency took charge of the entire situation, calling out all the troops and assuming control and direction of the troops and the police department.

The secrecy of the proceedings on the part of the men, and the frequently reiterated statement that the word "strike" had never been mentioned, made it impossible to have the troops on the scene before they actually got there.

A call can be made only when the riot or tumult is in existence or threatened, and it was not intended by the perpetrators of the betrayal of duty that there should be any notice given or any time for preparation for the emergency. The disorder that came that night was planned and intended, in order that the city might be so terrorized that a demand would come to recall the faithless officers on their own terms.

At the present time, when there is more or less talk about the men having been punished enough, it must be remembered that the men themselves still cling to their organization, show no indication of giving up their affiliation, and are doing everything in their power to prevent the recruiting of a loyal police force, and to sow the seeds of disloyalty among the men who are now being taken.

Present Situation.

The Police Commissioner is filling his police force as rapidly as possible. He has sent to the Civil Service Commission for a non-competitive examination a sufficient number of men to fill the vacancies. Every possible method has been used to prevent the recruiting of this force. Misapprehensions were created. Men were deterred from applying because they were made to think that the position was not going to be permanent, and applicants have been hounded both at the place of examination and at their homes. Every method has been employed to prevent the manufacture of uniforms, and time has necessarily been lost by the actions of these former patrolmen and their supporters who have succeeded, not in preventing the uniforms being made, and made by well-paid labor, but in a certain amount of delay and the sending out of the State of Massachusetts the money and the work that should be kept here for Massachusetts concerns and Massachusetts employees.

I have realized that the salaries in this department need revision, and I therefore make the following recommendations in regard to salaries that are fixed by statute: —

THE SUPERINTENDENT.

Since the salary of the superintendent was fixed in 1906, there has been no change, yet the duties have become arduous and will increase rather than diminish in the years to come. If $5,000 was considered a proper compensation in 1906, a much larger salary must be paid to-day commensurate with the requirements and responsibilities of the office. I therefore recommend such increase, appending to this report a bill as required by chapter 131 of the General Acts of 1919.

The Secretary.

The secretary to the Commissioner has many duties beyond the ordinary secretarial position. Not only has he those duties, but a large part of the administration of the Commissioner's office devolves upon him. He must be not only a good executive, but also a well-equipped attorney, for it is to him that the department must go for all legal services and legal advices. He must appear in various kinds of litigation, as, for instance, the disposition of property coming into the possession of the police by process of law where there are many claimants and frequent suits. He defends police officers sued civilly for causes arising out of the performance of their duty. He must sometimes appear for the prosecution in cases where the decision is of importance to the department. He has to hear and cause to be investigated and report on all cases where there is discussion concerning any license that the department issues. He must conduct cases before the trial board where the accused patrolman comes with counsel. The salary as fixed by the act of 1906 is inadequate, and feeling that it should be increased, I recommend legislation accordingly and append to this report a bill as required by chapter 131 of the General Acts of 1919.

Counsel.

The Commissioner may spend $3,500 per year for legal counsel. .The events of the past few months have demonstrated that it is possible for that sum to be inadequate in certain contingencies, and the department should not be so crippled. In the matter in which the Commissioner was obliged to seek outside counsel this year, the counsel secured considered it so vital to the whole State and Nation that he felt it his duty as a citizen to give his services for a mere nominal fee. The Hon. Herbert Parker charged but a nominal fee of $50, and charged that merely because he felt that it was necessary in order that the relation of counsel and client be established. Nevertheless, he postponed all his other affairs to the matter in which the department was concerned, and was constantly available for any service required. This report would not be complete or just without the grateful acknowledgment of the Commissioner and the department to him. The city and State are under a debt to him. The sum allowed for counsel fees, however, might easily in any one year be inadequate for the exigencies of this department, and I recommend that there be allowed the sum of $7,000, and append to this report a bill as required by chapter 131 of the General Acts of 1919.

Respect for the Symbol of the Law.

It is regrettable that the following recommendation is necessary, but when men wearing the uniform of the law showed it disrespect it is hardly to be wondered at that others in the community should do likewise. I find it incumbent on me to ask that there be incorporated into the statute law a provision compelling a respect for the uniform and office of a policeman. In the General Acts of 1917, chapter 327, Part I, section 56, the soldier is protected from abuse and insult. I ask for the same safeguard for the members of all the police forces of the State, and append to this report a bill as required by chapter 131 of the General Acts of 1919.

Pensions.

The Police Commissioner may at the present time retire from active service and place upon a pension any member of the police department who has served for twenty years and who is incapacitated for any cause. He cannot do so, however, without the request of the member himself, so that in cases which may arise where the member is clearly incapacitated and declines to make the request the only method of dispensing with his services is to remove him for inefficiency, — a rather harsh method. I therefore recommend that chapter 353 of the Acts of 1892 be so changed that the Police Commissioner may retire a man so incapacitated, and submit a bill as required by chapter 131 of the General Acts of 1919.

The Commissioner gratefully acknowledges the efficient and important services gratuitously rendered to him in matters of law by Thomas W. Proctor, Esq.

It would hardly be fitting that this annual report should be submitted without due and proper acknowledgment made to the individuals and organizations serving to protect the city when the police force was depleted. A splendid body of citizens enrolled themselves as volunteer policemen, serving, and willing to serve, without compensation or expectation of any; willing to undergo the hardships and the dangers of such service, and neglectful of their own interests and pursuits. To them this department owes a debt of gratitude for the service so unselfishly undertaken and splendidly performed, and for the department I thank them.

The whole community is now aware of the promptness with which the Massachusetts State Guard was mobilized, and the effectiveness with which it worked when it came into the city. I cannot add anything to the universal chorus of commendation that has greeted their work. But I can and do express the gratitude of the police department and the citizens of Boston to the citizen soldiery that preserved law and order here. It was indeed a pleasure to be in daily official communication with the leader of the troops, Brig.-Gen. Samuel D. Parker. He gave unsparingly of his time and his talents, and was of the greatest possible assistance to me throughout the whole situation. I desire to express to him publicly my appreciation of his admirable handling of the situation. He co-operated with this department in every particular, and with the fullest harmony, and from him, his officers and his troops the department has learned many things of value which will make for a more efficient and better-equipped police force. General Parker and the Massachusetts State Guard can rightly claim no little share in building up and starting on its road the police force that now protects the city.

EDWIN U. CURTIS,
Police Commissioner for the City of Boston.

BILLS SUBMITTED.

AN ACT RELATIVE TO THE SALARY OF THE SUPERINTENDENT OF POLICE OF THE CITY OF BOSTON.

SECTION 1. Section thirteen of chapter two hundred and ninety-one of the acts of the year nineteen hundred and six is hereby amended by striking out, in the tenth line, after the word "police", the comma, and inserting in place thereof a period; by striking out, in the tenth and eleventh lines, the words "which shall not exceed five thousand dollars per annum", and by inserting in the ninth line thereof, after the word "action", the words: — with the approval of the governor, — so that the same may read as follows: — *Section 13*. Except as authorized by the mayor of said city said commissioner shall not appoint any greater number of patrolmen than the present board of police of the said city is now authorized to appoint, nor shall the pay of the members of the police force other than said police commissioner and superintendent of police be increased or diminished, except by the concurrent action of the said mayor and the said police commissioner. The police commissioner may, without such concurrent action, with the approval of the governor, fix the salary of the superintendent of police.

SECTION 2. This act shall take effect upon its passage.

AN ACT RELATIVE TO THE SALARY OF THE SECRETARY OF THE POLICE COMMISSIONER FOR THE CITY OF BOSTON.

SECTION 1. Section eight of chapter two hundred and ninety-one of the acts of the year nineteen hundred and six, as amended by chapter three hundred and seven of the Special Acts of the year nineteen hundred and seventeen, is hereby amended by striking out, in the third line, the words "three thousand dollars", and inserting in place thereof the words: — an amount which shall be fixed by the police commissioner with the approval of the governor, — so that the same may read as follows: — *Section 8*. The annual salary of the police commissioner shall be eight thousand dollars, and of the secretary an amount which shall be fixed by the police commissioner with the approval of the governor, which shall be paid in monthly instalments by the city of Boston. Subject to the approval of the governor and council the police commissioner shall be provided with such rooms, which shall be suitably furnished, as shall be convenient and suitable for the performance of his duty, the expense of which shall be paid by the city of Boston.

SECTION 2. This act shall take effect upon its passage.

AN ACT RELATIVE TO THE EMPLOYMENT OF LEGAL ASSISTANCE BY THE POLICE COMMISSIONER FOR THE CITY OF BOSTON.

SECTION 1. Section nine of chapter two hundred and ninety-one of the acts of the year nineteen hundred and six is hereby amended by striking out in the fourth line thereof the words "thirty-five hundred dollars", and inserting in place thereof the words: — seven thousand dollars, — so that the same may read as follows: — *Section 9.* Said police commissioner may employ such legal assistance as he may deem necessary in the performance of his duty, and may incur expense therefor to an amount not exceeding seven thousand dollars in any municipal year, which expense shall be paid by the city of Boston upon the requisition of said police commissioner.

SECTION 2. This act shall take effect upon its passage.

AN ACT TO PROVIDE A PENALTY FOR INTERRUPTING, MOLESTING, INSULTING OR OBSTRUCTING A POLICE OFFICER WHILE IN PERFORMANCE OF DUTY.

Whoever interrupts, molests or insults, by abusive words or behavior, or obstructs any police officer while on duty or in the performance of his duty shall be punished by imprisonment for not more than six months or by a fine of not more than one hundred dollars.

AN ACT RELATIVE TO THE PENSIONING OF MEMBERS OF THE POLICE DEPARTMENT OF THE CITY OF BOSTON.

SECTION 1. Section one of chapter three hundred and fifty-three of the acts of the year eighteen hundred and ninety-two is hereby amended by striking out in the second line thereof the words "at his own request", so that the same may read as follows: — *Section 1.* The board of police of the city of Boston may retire from active service and place upon a pension roll any member of the police department who has performed faithful service in said department for a period not less than twenty years, if in the judgment of the board said officer is incapacitated for useful service on said force, and said board shall retire from such service and place upon a pension roll any member of said force who has arrived at the age of sixty-five years, or any member who shall be certified to said board in writing, by the physician to the board of health of said city, as being permanently incapacitated, either mentally or physically, by injury sustained in the actual performance of duty, from further performing duty as such member: *provided, however,* that no officer shall be retired under the provisions of this act unless such action is approved in writing by the mayor of the city of Boston; and *provided,* that soldiers and sailors who served during the war of the rebellion and who have received an honorable discharge shall not be retired at the age of sixty-five years except at their own request.

SECTION 2. This act shall take effect upon its passage.

THE DEPARTMENT.

The police department is at present constituted as follows: —

Police Commissioner.   Secretary.   2

The Police Force.

Superintendent,	1	Lieutenants,		41
Deputy superintendent,	1	Sergeants,		125
Chief inspector,	1	Patrolmen,		1,343
Captains,	27			
Inspectors,	28	Total,		1,568
Inspector of carriages (lieutenant),	1			

Signal Service.

Director,	1	Linemen,		6
Foreman,	1	Driver,		1
Signalmen,	6			
Mechanics,	3	Total,		18

Employees of the Department.

Clerks,	18	Foreman of stable,		1
Stenographers,	4	Hostlers,		9
Matrons of house of detention,	5	Assistant steward of city prison,		1
Matrons of station houses,	7	Janitors,		17
Engineers on police steamers,	3	Janitresses,		16
Firemen on police steamers,	7	Telephone operators,		3
Van drivers,	2	Total,		93

Recapitulation.

Police Commissioner and secretary,	2
Police force,	1,568
Signal service,	18
Employees,	93
Grand total,	1,681

DISTRIBUTION AND CHANGES.

The distribution of the police force is shown by Table 1. During the year 98 patrolmen were promoted from reserve men; 12 patrolmen and 6 reserve men were reinstated; 1,018 patrolmen were appointed; 41 patrolmen were discharged; 1,117 patrolmen abandoned their positions; 43 patrolmen and 2 reserve men resigned; 1 inspector, 2 lieutenants, 1 sergeant and 9 patrolmen were retired on pension; 1 captain, 2 inspectors, 2 lieutenants and 11 patrolmen died. (See Tables II, III, IV, VI.)

POLICE OFFICERS INJURED WHILE ON DUTY.

The following statement shows the number of police officers injured while on duty during the past year, the number of duties lost by them on account thereof, and the causes of the injuries: —

HOW INJURED.	Number of Men injured.	Number of Duties lost.
In arresting prisoners, ...	39	626
In pursuing criminals, ...	15	237
By stopping runaways, ...	1	44
By cars and other vehicles at crossings, . .	9	548
Various other causes, ...	62	440
Totals, ...	126	1,895

WORK OF THE DEPARTMENT.

Arrests.

The total number of persons arrested, counting each arrest as that of a separate person, was 67,947 as against 90,293 the preceding year, being a decrease of 22,346. The percentage of decrease and increase was as follows: —

		Per Cent.
Offences against the person, ...	Decrease,	5.03
Offences against property committed with violence,	Increase,	13.83
Offences against property committed without violence, ...	Decrease,	5.19
Malicious offences against property, ...	Increase,	10.60
Forgery and offences against the currency, . .	Increase,	43.55
Offences against the license laws, ...	Increase,	22.51
Offences against chastity, morality, etc., . . .	Decrease,	40.76
Offences not included in the foregoing, . . .	Decrease,	27.03

There were 7,402 persons arrested on warrants and 49,253 without warrants; 11,292 persons were summoned by the court; 64,715 persons were held for trial; 2,595 were released from custody; and 637 were delivered to United States authorities. The number of males arrested was 62,280; of females, 5,667; of foreigners, 24,776, or approximately 36.46 per cent; of minors, 9,660. Of the total number arrested, 27,325, or 40.21 per cent, were nonresidents. (See Tables X, XI.)

The nativity of the prisoners was as follows: —

United States, . . .	43,171	East Indies, . . .	6
British Provinces, . .	3,780	West Indies, . . .	83
Ireland, ...	7,694	Turkey, ...	125
England, ...	973	South America, . . .	41
France, ...	152	Switzerland, . . .	9
Germany, ...	262	Belgium, ...	63
Italy, ...	3,210	Armenia, ...	32
Russia, ...	4,700	Africa, ...	8
China, ...	272	Hungary, ...	17
Greece, ...	400	Asia, ...	19
Sweden, ...	887	Arabia, ...	1
Scotland, ...	591	Mexico, ...	6
Spain, ...	78	Japan, ...	10
Norway, ...	239	Syria, ...	121
Poland, ...	208	Roumania, . . .	7
Australia, ...	28	Lithuania, . . .	3
Austria, ...	187	Egypt, ...	2
Portugal, ...	195	Philippine Islands, . .	1
Finland, ...	235	Cuba, ...	2
Denmark, ...	70		
Holland, ...	44	Total, . . .	67,947
Wales, ...	15		

The number of arrests for the year was 67,947, being a decrease of 22,346 from last year, and 26,731 less than the average for the past five years. There were 35,540 persons arrested for drunkenness, being 19,408 less than last year, and 26,533 less than the average for the past five years. Of the arrests for drunkenness this year there was a decrease of 35.40 per cent in males, and a decrease of 34.26 per cent in females from last year. (See Tables XI, XIII.)

Of the total number of arrests for the year (67,947), 525 were for violations of the city ordinances; that is to say, 1 arrest in 129 was for such offence, or .77 per cent.

Fifty-four and fifty-six one-hundredths per cent of the persons taken into custody were between the ages of twenty and forty. (See Table XII.)

The number of persons punished by fines was 12,225, and the fines amounted to $107,325. (See Table XIII.)

Sixty-two persons were committed to the State Prison, 2,240 to the House of Correction, 73 to the Women's Prison, 104 to the Reformatory Prison and 1,235 to other institutions. The total years of imprisonment were 1 life, 428 indefinite, 2,214 years, 8 months; the total number of days' attendance at court by officers was 30,274; and the witness fees earned by them amounted to $8,493.35.

The value of property taken from prisoners and lodgers was $226,262.62.

Thirty-five witnesses were detained at station houses; 56 were accommodated with lodgings, a decrease of 21 from last year. There was a decrease of 5.04 per cent from last year in the number of insane persons taken in charge, a decrease of about 17.80 per cent in the number of sick and injured persons assisted, and a decrease of about 6.91 per cent in the number of lost children cared for.

The average amount of property stolen in the city for the five years from 1915 to 1919, inclusive, was $536,066.52; in 1919 it was $1,415,485.79, or $879,419.27 more than the average. The amount of property stolen in and out of the city which was recovered by the Boston police was $1,238,206.26, as against $578,890.63 last year, or $659,315.63 **more.**

The average amount of fines imposed by the courts for the five years from 1915 to 1919, inclusive, was $113,364.50; in 1919 it was $107,325, or $6,039.50 less than the average.

The average number of days' attendance at court was 41,973; in 1919 it was 30,274, or 11,699 less than the average. The average amount of witness fees earned was $11,771.74; in 1919 it was 8,493.35, or $3,278.39 less than the average. (See Table XIII.)

Drunkenness.

In arrests for drunkenness the average per day was 97. There were 19,408 fewer persons arrested than in 1918, a decrease of 35.32 per cent; 50.99 per cent of the arrested persons were nonresidents, and 40.58 per cent were of foreign birth. (See Table XI.)

Bureau of Criminal Investigation.

The "identification room" now contains 57,801 photographs, 50,603 of which are photographs with Bertillon measurements, a system used by the department for the past twenty years. In accordance with the Revised Laws, chapter 225, sections 18 and 21, we are allowed photographs with Bertillon measurements taken of convicts in the State Prison and reformatory, a number of which have already been added to our Bertillon cabinets. This, together with the adoption of the system by the department in 1898, is and will continue to be of great assistance in the identification of criminals. A large number of important identifications have thus been made during the year for this and other police departments, through which the sentences in many instances have been materially increased. The records of 735 criminals have been added to the records in this Bureau, which now contains a total of 41,836. The number of cases reported at this office which have been investigated during the year is 7,528. There are 32,927 cases reported on the assignment books kept for this purpose, and reports made on these cases are filed away for future reference. The system of indexing adopted by this Bureau for the use of the department now contains a list of records, histories, photographs, dates of arrest, etc., of about 175,000 persons. There are also "histories and press clippings," now numbering 8,126, made by this Bureau, in envelope form for police reference.

The finger-print system of identification which was adopted in June, 1906, has progressed in a satisfactory manner, and with it the identification of criminals is facilitated. It has become very useful in tracing criminals and furnishing corroborating evidence in many instances.

The statistics of the work of this branch of the service are included in the statement of the general work of the department, but as the duties are of a special character the following statement will be of interest: —

Number of persons arrested, principally for felonies, . . . 1,573

Fugitives from justice from other States, arrested and delivered
  to officers from those States, ... 41

Number of cases investigated, ... 7,528

Number of extra duties performed, ... 2,503

Number of cases of homicide and supposed homicide investigated and evidence prepared for trial in court, ... 192

Number of cases of abortion and supposed abortion investigated
  and evidence prepared for court, ... 6

Number of days spent in court by officers, ... 3,065

Amount of stolen property recovered, . . . $417,759.68

Number of years' imprisonment imposed by court, 164 years, 10 months

Number of photographs added to "identification room," . . 2,898

Officer detailed to assist Medical Examiners.

The officer detailed to assist the medical examiners reports having investigated 844 cases of death from the following causes: —

Abortion, ...	5	Drowning, . . .	32
Aeroplane, ...	1	Electricity, . . .	2
Alcoholism, . . .	5	Elevators, . . .	9
Asphyxiation, . . .	2	Falling objects, . .	11
Automobiles, . . .	12	Falls, ...	53
Burns, ...	25	Heat, ...	2
Collapse of tank, . .	19	Kicked by horse, . .	1

Ladder truck, . . . 1	Suffocation, ... 6
Machinery, ... 6	Suicides, . . . 66
Natural causes, . . . 267	Teams, ... 8
Poison, ... 84	Homicides, ... 183
Railway (street), . . . 3	
Railroad (steam), . . . 33	Total, ... 844
Stillborn, ... 8	

On 330 of the above cases inquests were held.

Of the total number, the following homicide cases were prosecuted in the courts: —

Aeroplanes, ... 1	Neglect, ... 1
Asphyxiation, . . . 1	Poison, ... 2
Automobiles, ... 111	Railway (street), . . . 18
Boxing matches, . . . 1	Shooting (accidental), . . 2
Burns, ... 1	Shot resisting officer, . . 2
Collapse of tank, . . . 1	Shot in riot, ... 8
Elevators, ... 2	Suicides, ... 1
Falls, ... 1	Stick thrown, . . . 1
Manslaughter, . . . 14	Teams, ... 3
Motorcycle, ... 1	
Murder, ... 10	Total, ... 183
Natural causes, . . . 1	

Lost, Abandoned and Stolen Property.

On Dec. 1, 1918, there were 1,088 articles of lost, stolen or abandoned property in the custody of the property clerk; 1,117 were received during the year; 663 pieces were sold at public auction and the net proceeds, $955.78, were turned over to the chief clerk; 53 packages containing money to the amount of $239.02 were turned over to the chief clerk; one horse and wagon were sold at public auction and the net proceeds, $23.14, turned over to the chief clerk; 87 packages were delivered to owners, finders or administrators, leaving 1,401 on hand.

Special Events.

The following is a list of special events transpiring during the year, and gives the number of police detailed for duty at each: —

1918.   Men.

Dec. 7, Boston Opera House and Symphony Hall, British jubi-
    lation meeting, ... 70
Dec. 8, Meeting of Friends of Irish Freedom, ... 26
Dec. 11, Hoosac Dock, return of soldiers, ... 28
Dec. 12, North Station, Home Guard returning to Camp
    Devens, ... 94
Dec. 14, Funeral of Lieut. William J. Irwin, ... 45
Dec. 17, Funeral of Police Commissioner Stephen O'Meara, . 135
Dec. 18, Boston arena fire, ... 38
Dec. 19, Faneuil Hall, Italian American Red Cross meeting, . 24
Dec. 21, Dancing on Boston Common, auspices of Red Cross, . 18
Dec. 24, Boston Common, Christmas Eve celebration, . . 42
Dec. 24, Beacon Hill, Christmas Eve celebration, . . . 32
Dec. 24, Holy Cross Cathedral, midnight Mass, ... 22
Dec. 25, Beacon Hill, Christmas carol singing, ... 27
Dec. 31, Boston Common, New Year's Eve celebration, . . 17

1919.

Jan. 3, Faneuil Hall, meeting of Independent Workmen's
    Circle, ... 107
Jan. 15, North End, explosion of molasses tank, ... 190
Jan. 16, Scene of molasses tank explosion, ... 93
Jan. 17, Scene of molasses tank explosion, ... 93
Jan. 18, Scene of molasses tank explosion, ... 93
Jan. 19, Scene of molasses tank explosion, ... 93
Jan. 20, Scene of molasses tank explosion, ... 45
Jan. 21, Scene of molasses tank explosion, ... 45
Jan. 22, Scene of molasses tank explosion, ... 45
Jan. 23, Scene of molasses tank explosion, ... 45
Jan. 29 to Feb. 10, inclusive, special duty to district attorney's
    office, ... 260
Jan. 30, North Station, return of Harvard Unit from war, . 46
Feb. 3, Crawford House fire, ... 46
Feb. 5, Funeral of Inspector Thomas H. Lynch, ... 40
Feb. 5, South Station, returning wounded soldiers, . . . 40
Feb. 8, South Station, returning soldiers, ... 21
Feb. 9, South Station, returning soldiers, ... 8
Feb. 11, Naval parade, ... 342
Feb. 12, Jamaica Pond, ice carnival, ... 42
Feb. 24, Visit of President Wilson, parade and receptions, . . 1,542
Mar. 9, Wilbur Theatre, women's suffrage meeting, . . . 18
Mar. 19, Symphony Hall, Lodge-Lowell debate, ... 95
Mar. 23, Faneuil Hall, Civic Federation meeting, . . . 19
Apr. 3, Reception and parade, returning colored soldiers, . . 268
Apr. 4, Commonwealth Pier, returning soldiers, ... 30
Apr. 5, Commonwealth Pier, returning soldiers, ... 94

1919.		Men.
Apr. 6, Commonwealth Pier, debarkation of soldiers,	. .	48
Apr. 8, Commonwealth Pier, debarkation of soldiers,	. .	48
Apr. 15 to 21, inclusive, strike of telephone operators,	. .	385
Apr. 19, Marathon race, ...	. .	437
Apr. 20, Boston Common, reception to officers of 26th Division,		21
Apr. 20, Boston Opera House, Friends of Irish Freedom,	. .	19
Apr. 21, Boston Common, Liberty Loan drive,	. .	25
Apr. 25, Parade of 26th Division, ...	. .	1,372
Apr. 28, Franklin Field, airplanes arriving, .	. .	51
Apr. 29, Funeral of Inspector Alfred N. Douglas,	. .	40
May 1, Roxbury riot, ...	. .	248
May 3, South Boston, parade of returned soldiers,	. .	297
May 5, Liberty Loan drives, ...	. .	86
May 5, Funeral of Capt. Hugh J. Lee, . . .	. .	67
May 6, Franklin Field airplanes, ...	. .	62
May 8, East Armory, school cadet drill, . .	. .	17
May 10, Boston Common, Liberty Loan drive,	. .	16
May 10, Parade of Girl Scouts, ...	. .	43
May 15 and 16, Charlestown, reception to returned soldiers,	.	155
May 28, Parade of Jewish Conference, . . .	. .	364
May 30, Fire in Graham Paper Factory, South Boston,	. .	34
June 7, Brighton's reception to returned soldiers and sailors,	.	42
June 7, Boston Common, Junior Red Cross Field Day,	. .	60
June 7, Dorchester Day celebration, . . .	. .	87
June 8, Parade of National Polish Department of America,	.	370
June 10, Mechanics' Building, meeting of Friends of Irish Freedom, ...	. .	63
June 14, Boston Common, Flag Day exercises, .	. .	47
June 16, Charlestown, night before the 17th of June, .	. .	175
June 17, Anniversary of Battle of Bunker Hill, .	. .	373
June 19, Funeral of Patrolman Adolph F. Butterman,	.	56
June 28 to 30, inclusive, visit of President of Irish Republic,	.	277
June 30 to July 1, inclusive, visit of President of Brazil,	. .	80
July 2 to 11, inclusive, Market Teamsters' strike,	. .	153
July 4, Celebration, Independence Day, . .	. .	620
July 9, Funeral of Lieut. Albert F. Lovell, . .	. .	40
July 17, Strike of Boston Elevated Railway employees,	.	637
July 18, Strike of Boston Elevated Railway employees,	.	540
July 19, Strike of Boston Elevated Railway employees,	.	568
July 20, Strike of Boston Elevated Railway employees,	.	76
Aug. 26, Parade of Italian sailors, . . .	. .	57
Aug. 29, North End reception to Italian sailors, .	. .	39
Sept. 1, Labor Day parade, ...	. .	336
Oct. 5 and 6, Visit of King and Queen of Belgium, and visit of Cardinal Mercier, ...	. .	321
Oct. 11, Soldiers' Field, Harvard-Colby football game,	. .	20

1919.   **Men.**

Oct. 13, Columbus day parade, ...   146
Oct. 18, Soldiers' Field, Harvard-Brown football game,   .   .   25
Oct. 25, Soldiers' Field, Harvard-Penn football game,   .   .   25
Nov. 1, Soldiers' Field, Harvard-Springfield football game,   .   28
Nov. 4, State election, ...   240
Nov. 22, Stadium, Harvard-Yale football game, ...   128
Nov. 22, Braves' Field, Somerville-Everett high school football
    game, ...   22
Nov. 27, Stadium, 101st Engineers and 101st Field Artillery
    football game, ...   28

Miscellaneous Business.

	1916-17.	1917-18.	1918-19.
Abandoned children cared for, . . .	11	15	14
Accidents reported, ...	5,114	4,555	4,009
Buildings found open and made secure, .	2,790	3,034	3,459
Cases investigated, ...	26,857	26,804	29,482
Dangerous buildings reported, . .	19	32	16
Dangerous chimneys reported, . .	6	23	26
Dead bodies cared for, . . .	435	384	303
Dead bodies recovered, . . .	64	30	28
Defective bulkheads reported, . .	–	–	11
Defective cesspools reported, . .	232	124	90
Defective catch basin reported, . .	–	1	–
Defective drains and vaults reported, .	18	15	28
Defective fences reported, . . .	3	1	–
Defective fire alarms and clocks reported,	4	4	1
Defective gas pipes reported, . .	–	–	47
Defective hydrants reported, . .	151	173	88
Defective lamps reported, . . .	5,592	650,906	29,148
Defective water meters reported, . .	1	7	–
Defective sewers reported, . .	162	85	75

MISCELLANEOUS BUSINESS — *Concluded.*

	1916–17.	1917–18.	1918–19.
Defective signs reported, ...	8	16	–
Defective streets and sidewalks reported,	8,812	8,192	8,545
Defective wires reported, ...	–	9	1
Defective trees reported, ...	27	4	1
Defective water gates and shutoffs reported.	10	19	–
Defective water pipes reported, . .	182	244	119
Defective water fountains reported, .	–	1	–
Disturbances suppressed, ...	654	424	565
Extra duties performed, ...	50,810	43,175	42,057
Fire alarms given, ...	2,056	2,449	2,676
Fires extinguished, ...	991	1,232	974
Insane persons taken in charge, . .	477	436	414
Intoxicated persons assisted, . .	27	15	12
Junk dealers investigated, ...	–	–	1
Lost children restored, ...	1,821	1,977	1,859
Missing persons reported, ...	506	529	567
Missing persons found, ...	191	250	262
Pawnbrokers investigated, . . .	–	–	4
Persons rescued from drowning, . .	22	16	12
Private detectives investigated, . .	–	–	5
Second-hand dealers investigated, . .	–	–	4
Sick and injured persons assisted, . .	7,533	6,320	5,195
Stray teams reported and put up, . .	158	130	82
Street obstructions removed, . . .	2,377	1,854	1,185
Water running to waste reported, . .	562	984	485
Witnesses detained, ...	60	71	35

INSPECTOR OF CLAIMS.

The officer detailed to assist the committee on claims and law department in investigating claims against the city for alleged damage of various kinds reports that he investigated 1,497 cases, 7 of which were on account of damage done by dogs.

Other Services performed.

Number of cases investigated,	1,497
Number of witnesses examined,	7,537
Number of notices served,	4,383
Number of permissions granted,	5,679
Number of days in court,	122
Number of cases settled on recommendation from this office,	55
Collected for damage to the city's property and paid bills amounting to,	$474.50

HOUSE OF DETENTION.

The house of detention for women is located in the court house, Somerset Street. All the women arrested in the city proper are taken to the house of detention in vans provided for the purpose. They are then held in charge of the matron until the next session of the court before which they are to appear. If sentenced to imprisonment, they are returned to the house of detention, and from there conveyed to the jail or institution to which they have been sentenced.

During the year there were 4,055 women committed for the following: —

Drunkenness,	1,921
Larceny,	388
Nightwalking,	68
Fornication,	208
Being idle and disorderly,	103
Assault and battery,	11
Adultery,	35
Violation of the liquor law,	2
Keeping a house of ill fame,	8
Witness,	2
County jail,	852
Municipal court,	137
Various other offences,	320
Total,	4,055

POLICE SIGNAL SERVICE.

Signal Boxes.

The total number of boxes in use is 504. Of these, 325 are connected with the underground system and 179 with the overhead.

Miscellaneous Work.

During the year the employees of this service responded to 1,334 trouble calls; inspected 504 signal boxes, 18 signal desks and 955 batteries; repaired 64 box movements, 11 registers, 17 polar box bells, 43 locks, 20 time stamps, 4 gongs, 1 stable motor, 2 stable registers, 4 vibrator bells, besides repairing all bell and electric light work at headquarters and the various stations. There have been made 5 plungers, 10 complete box fittings, 8 line blocks, 15 old style box movements, and a large amount of small work done that cannot be classified. A new register was built from an old "Boston style" register for Station 18, so that theirs might be repaired.

The following boxes have been installed underground: 1 at Station 10, 1 at Station 11 and 1 at Station 14. Again this department had to rearrange the fourth circuit at Station 11, to clear the 1919 underground district on Pleasant and Hancock streets, as there were no ducts, and an extra cable was laid in Adams Street from the station to Eaton Square.

There are in use in the signal service 3 horses, 5 patrol wagons and 1 pung.

During the year the wagons made 35,772 runs, covering an aggregate distance of 43,851 miles. There were 35,353 prisoners conveyed to the station houses, 1,942 runs were made to take injured or insane persons to station houses, the hospitals or their homes; and 438 runs were made to take lost children to station houses. There were 947 runs to fires and 24 runs for liquor seizures. During the year there were 504 signal boxes in use arranged on 72 battery circuits and 70 telephone circuits; 568,731 telephone messages and 3,522,508 "on duty" calls were sent over the lines.

The following list comprises the property in the signal service at the present time: —

18 signal desks.	47,923 feet of duct.
72 circuits.	61 manholes.
504 street signal boxes.	1 buggy.
14 stable call boards.	1 line wagon.
81 test boxes.	1 express wagon.
955 cells of battery.	1 mugwump wagon.
589,044 feet underground cable.	1 traverse pung.
239,550 feet overhead cable.	1 caravan.

HARBOR SERVICE.

The special duties performed by the police of Division 8, comprising the harbor and the islands therein, were as follows: —

Value of property recovered, consisting of boats, rigging, float-stages, etc.,	$59,081.89
Vessels from foreign ports boarded,	516
Vessels ordered from the channel,	734
Vessels removed from the channel by police steamers,	11
Assistance rendered vessels,	85
Assistance rendered to wharfingers,	2
Permits granted to discharge cargoes from vessels at anchor,	48
Obstructions removed from channel,	46
Alarms of fire on the water front attended,	35
Fires extinguished without alarm,	2
Boats challenged,	1,177
Sick and injured persons assisted,	10
Dead bodies recovered,	23
Dead bodies cared for,	3
Persons rescued from drowning,	2
Vessels assigned to anchorage,	470
Cases investigated,	1,393

The number of vessels that arrived in this port during the year was 7,241, 6,318 being from domestic ports, 407 from the British provinces and 516 from foreign ports. Of the latter, 485 were steamers, 2 ships, 18 barks and 11 schooners.

A patrol service was maintained in Dorchester Bay from June 23 to October 16. The launch "Alert" cruised nightly from Castle Island to Neponset bridge. Three hundred and twenty-nine boats were challenged; 122 cases investigated; and assistance rendered to 9 boats in distress by reason of disabled engines, stress of weather, etc. From these boats 23 persons whose lives were in jeopardy were rescued, and property to the value of $3,800 was saved from destruction.

Horses.

On the 30th of November, 1918, there were 38 horses in the service. During the year five were purchased, five delivered to the State Department of Health, four sold and three humanely killed. At the present time there are 31 in the service, as shown by Table IX.

Vehicle Service.

Automobiles.

There are 38 automobiles in the service at the present time: four attached to headquarters; one at the house of detention, used as a woman's van and kept at Division 4; six in the city proper and attached to Divisions 1, 2, 3, 4 and 5; four in the South Boston district, attached to Divisions 6 and 12; two in the East Boston district attached to Division 7; five in the Roxbury district attached to Divisions 9 and 10; three in the Dorchester district, attached to Division 11; two in the Jamaica Plain district, attached to Division 13; three in the Brighton district, attached to Division 14; one in the Charlestown district, attached to Division 15; two in the Back Bay and Fenway, attached to Division 16; two in the West Roxbury district attached to Division 17; two in the Mattapan district, attached to Division 19; and one unassigned.

Cost of Running Automobiles.

Repairs, ...	$11,819 33
Tires, ...	6,777 99
Gasoline, ...	7,507 60
Oil, ...	641 11
Rent of garage, ...	467 55
License fees, ...	98 00
Total, ...	$27,311 58

Ambulances.

The department is equipped with combination automobiles (patrol and ambulance) located in Divisions 1, 3, 4, 5, 6, 7, 9, 10, 11, 12, 13, 14, 15, 16, 17 and 19; also ambulances located in Divisions 1 and 13.

During the year the ambulances responded to calls to convey sick and injured persons to the following places: —

City Hospital, ...	1,598
City Hospital (Relief Station, Haymarket Square), . . .	764
City Hospital (Relief Station, East Boston), . . .	202
Calls where services were not required, ...	189
Home, ...	113
Massachusetts General Hospital, ...	97
St. Elizabeth's Hospital, ...	57
Morgue, ...	49
Boston State Hospital (including 40 to Psychopathic Department), ...	41
Police station houses, ...	18
Peter Bent Brigham Hospital, ...	10
Forest Hills Hospital, ...	6
Faulkner Hospital, ...	4
Lying-in Hospital, ...	4
Carney Hospital, ...	2
Homœopathic Hospital, ...	1
Massachusetts Eye and Ear Infirmary, ...	1
St. Mary's Infant Asylum, ...	1
State Armory (south), ...	1
Total, ...	3,158

List of Vehicles used by the Department.

DIVISIONS.	Combination Auto and Ambulance.	Patrol Wagons.	Other Wagons.	Automobiles.	Pung.	Vans.	Ambulances.	Buggies.	Sleigh.	Motor Van.	Motor Cycles.	Motor Cycle Side-cars.	Totals.
Headquarters,	–	–	–	4	–	–	–	–	–	–	–	–	4
Division 1,	1	–	–	–	–	–	1	–	–	–	–	–	2
Division 2,	–	–	–	1	–	–	–	–	–	–	–	–	1
Division 3,	1	–	–	–	–	–	–	–	–	–	–	–	1
Division 4,	1	–	–	–	–	–	–	–	–	1	–	–	2
Division 5,	1	–	–	1	–	–	–	–	–	–	–	–	2
Division 6,	1	–	–	1	–	–	–	–	–	–	–	–	2
Division 7,	1	–	–	1	–	–	–	–	–	–	–	–	2
Division 9,	1	–	–	1	–	–	–	–	–	–	–	–	2
Division 10,	2	–	–	1	–	–	–	–	–	–	–	–	3
Division 11,	2	1	–	1	–	–	–	–	–	–	–	–	4
Division 12,	1	–	–	1	–	–	–	–	–	–	2	–	4
Division 13,	1	1	–	1	–	–	1	–	1	–	–	–	5
Division 14,	1	–	–	2	–	–	–	–	–	–	2	1	6
Division 15,	1	–	–	–	–	–	–	–	–	–	–	–	1
Division 16,	1	–	–	1	–	–	–	–	–	–	6	3	11
Division 17,	1	–	–	1	–	–	–	–	–	–	–	–	2
Division 18,	–	1	–	–	–	–	–	–	–	–	–	–	1
Division 19,	1	–	–	1	–	–	–	–	–	–	2	–	4
Joy Street stable,	–	2	6	–	1	4	3	2	–	–	–	–	18
Unassigned,	1	–	–	–	–	–	–	–	–	–	–	–	1
Totals,	19	5	6	18	1	4	5	2	1	1	12	4	78

Public Carriages.

During the year there were 1,631 carriage licenses granted, being an increase of 12 as compared with last year; 1,132 motor carriages were licensed, being an increase of 87 compared with last year.

There has been a decrease of 320 in the number of horse-drawn licensed carriages during the year.

There were 73 articles, consisting of umbrellas, coats, handbags, etc., left in carriages during the year, which were turned over to the inspector; 48 of these were restored to the owners, and the balance placed in the keeping of the lost property bureau.

The following statement gives details concerning public hackney carriages, as well as licenses to drive the same: —

Number of applications for carriage licenses received, .	1,642
Number of carriages licensed, .	1,631
Number of licenses transferred,	158
Number of licenses canceled or revoked,	62
Number of carriages inspected,	1,631
Applications for drivers' licenses reported upon, .	1,867
Number of complaints against drivers investigated,	192
Number of warrants obtained, .	14
Number of days spent in court,	17
Articles left in carriages reported by citizens,	43
Articles found in carriages reported by drivers,	73
Drivers' applications for licenses rejected,	9

Since July 1, 1914, the Police Commissioner has assigned to persons or corporations licensed to set up and use hackney carriages places designated as special stands for such licensed carriages, and there have been issued in the year ending Nov. 30, 1919, 495 such special stands.

Of these special stands there have been 42 canceled and 2 transferred.

Sight-seeing Automobiles.

During the year ending Nov. 30, 1919, there have been issued licenses for 24 sight-seeing automobiles and 21 special stands for them. There have been 42 chauffeurs' licenses granted.

WAGON LICENSES.

Licenses are granted to persons or corporations to set up and use trucks, wagons or other vehicles to convey merchandise from place to place within the city for hire.

During the year 5,204 applications for such licenses were received; 5,201 of these were granted and 3 rejected.

Of these licenses 70 were subsequently canceled for nonpayment of license fee, 22 for other causes, and 25 transferred to new locations. (See Tables XIV, XVI.)

LISTING MALE RESIDENTS OF BOSTON, ETC.

YEAR.	May Canvass.	YEAR.	May Canvass.
1903, ...	181,045	1912,[1] . . .	214,178
1904, ...	193,195	1913,[1] . . .	215,388
1905, ...	194,547	1914,[1] . . .	219,364
1906, ...	195,446	1915,[1] . . .	220,883
1907, ...	195,900	1916, ...	−[2]
1908, ...	201,255	1917,[1] . . .	221,207
1909, ...	201,391	1918,[1] . . .	224,012
1910,[1]	203,603	1919,[1] . . .	227,466
1911,[1]	206,825		

Women Voters verified.

1903, ...	14,611	1912, ...	10,567
1904, ...	15,633	1913, ...	9,686
1905, ...	14,591	1914, ...	8,963
1906, ...	13,427	1915, ...	8,253
1907, ...	12,822	1916, ...	−[2]
1908, ...	11,915	1917, ...	9,291
1909, ...	11,048	1918, ...	18,950
1910, ...	10,486	1919, ...	17,289
1911, ...	9,935		

[1] Changed to April 1.   [2] Listing done by assessors.

Listing Expenses.

The expenses of listing residents, not including the services rendered by members of the police force, were as follows: —

Printing,	$14,569 48
Clerical service,	12,250 00
Stationery,	308 80
Interpreters,	480 63
Teaming,	24 00
Telephone,	14 66
Total,	$27,647 57

Number of Policemen employed in Listing.

April 1,	1,227
April 2,	1,086
April 3,	730
April 4,	290
April 5,	53
April 7,	5
April 8,	1

SPECIAL POLICE.

Special police officers are appointed to serve without pay from the city, on the written application of any officer or board in charge of a department of the city of Boston, or on the application of any responsible corporation or person, such a corporation or person to be liable for the official misconduct of the person appointed.

During the year ending Nov. 30, 1919, there were 3,142 special police officers appointed; 15 applications for appointment were refused for cause and 2 revoked.

Appointments were made on applications received, as follows: —

From United States government,	193
From State departments,	32
From city departments,	395
From county of Suffolk,	20

From railroad corporations, ... 220
From other corporations or associations, ... 1,954
From theatres and other places of amusement, . . . 256
From private institutions, ... 60
From churches, ... 12
                                                    ——
Total, ... 3,142

RAILROAD POLICE.

There were 136 persons appointed railroad policemen during the year, 78 of whom were employees of the New York, New Haven & Hartford Railroad, 55 of the Boston & Maine Railroad, 1 of the Boston, Revere Beach & Lynn Railroad, and 2 of the New York Central Railroad.

MISCELLANEOUS LICENSES.

The total number of applications for miscellaneous licenses received was 20,339; of these, 20,245 were granted, of which 117 were canceled for nonpayment, leaving 20,128 issued. During the year 227 applications were transferred, 94 rejected, 1,956 canceled and 30 revoked. The officers investigated 306 complaints arising under these licenses. The fees collected and paid into the city treasury amounted to $41,179.50. (See Table XIV.)

MUSICIANS' LICENSES.

Itinerant.

During the year there were 63 applications for itinerant musicians' licenses received, all of which were granted. Three licenses were subsequently canceled on account of nonpayment of the license fee.

All the instruments in use by itinerant musicians are inspected before the license is granted, and it is arranged by a qualified musician, not a member of the department, that such instruments shall be inspected in April and September of each year.

During the year 108 instruments were inspected, with the following results: —

KIND OF INSTRUMENT.	Number inspected.	Number passed.	Number rejected.
Street pianos, ...	60	50	10
Hand organs, ...	21	13	8
Violins, ...	8	8	–
Harps, ...	3	3	–
Flutes, ...	3	3	–
Accordions, ...	4	4	–
Guitars, ...	4	4	–
Banjos, ...	3	3	–
Mandolins, ...	2	2	–
Totals, ...	108	90	18

Collective.

Collective musicians' licenses are granted to bands of persons over sixteen years of age to play on musical instruments in company with designated processions at stated times and places.

The following shows the number of applications made for these licenses during the last five years, and the action taken thereon: —

YEAR.	Applications.	Granted.	Rejected.
1915, ...	253	250	3
1916, ...	262	261	1
1917, ...	265	265	–
1918, ...	225	224	1
1919, ...	224	220	4

CARRYING DANGEROUS WEAPONS.

The following return shows the number of applications made to the Police Commissioner for licenses to carry loaded pistols or revolvers in this Commonwealth during the past five years, the number of such applications granted, the number refused and the number revoked: —

YEAR.	Applications.	Granted.	Rejected.	Revoked.
1915, . , . .	1,556	1,425	131	–
1916, ...	1,384	1,301	83	–
1917, ...	2,719	2,583	136	–
1918, ...	2,463	2,374	89	3
1919, ...	5,006	4,539	467	4

PUBLIC LODGING HOUSES.

The following shows the number of public lodging houses licensed by the Police Commissioner under chapter 242 of the Acts of 1904 during the year, the location of each house and the number of lodgers accommodated: —

LOCATION.	Number lodged.	LOCATION.	Number lodged.
19 Causeway Street, . .	6,779	120 Eliot Street, ...	52,999
164 Commercial Street, . .	16,752	1025 Washington Street, . .	36,499
194 Commercial Street, . .	36,083	1051 Washington Street, . .	68,581
234 Commercial Street, . .	18,655	1202 Washington Street, . .	55,084
238 Commercial Street, . .	31,959	Total, ...	360,738
17 Davis Street, . . .	37,347		

PENSIONS AND BENEFITS.

On Dec. 1, 1918, there were 232 pensioners on the roll. During the year 14 died, viz., 1 inspector, 2 lieutenants, 10 patrolmen and a signal service driver; and 18 were added, viz., 1 inspector, 2 lieutenants, 1 sergeant, 9 patrolmen, the director of the signal service, a signal service painter, and the widows of Patrolmen Brennan, Butterman and Deininger, leaving 236 on the roll at date, including the widows of 24 policemen and the mother of 1 policeman who died of injuries received in the service.

The payments on account of pensions during the past year amounted to $152,439.24, and it is estimated that $168,-609.16 will be required for pensions in 1920. This does not include pensions for 2 captains, 1 sergeant and 8 patrolmen, all of whom are sixty-five or over, and are entitled to be pensioned on account of age and term of service.

The invested fund of the police charitable fund on the thirtieth day of November last amounted to $207,550. There are 72 beneficiaries at the present time, and there has been paid to them the sum of $7,940 during the past year.

The invested fund of the Police Relief Association on the thirtieth day of November was $203,532.97.

FINANCIAL.

The total expenditures for police purposes during the past year, including the pensions, house of detention, station house matrons and listing persons twenty years of age or more, but exclusive of the maintenance of the police signal service, were $2,832,675.88. (See Table XVII.)

The total revenue paid into the city treasury from fees from licenses over which the police have supervision, for the sale of unclaimed and condemned property, uniform cloth, etc., was $60,398.64. (See Table XIV.)

The cost of maintaining the police signal service during the year was $72,111.59. (See Table XVIII.)

Statistical Tables.

Table I.

Distribution of Police Force, Signal Service and Employees, Nov. 30, 1919.

RANK OR POSITION	Headquarters	1	2	3	4	5	6	7	8	9	10	11	12	13	14	15	16	17	18	19	Traffic Police	Signal Service	House of Detention	Totals
										Divisions.														
Police Commissioner,	1																							1
Secretary,	1																							1
Superintendent,	1																							1
Deputy superintendent,	1																							1
Chief inspector,	1																							1
Captains,	8	1	1	1	1	1	1	1	1	1	1	1	1	1	1	1	1	1	1	1				27
Inspectors,	25					1				1	1													28
Lieutenants,	4	2	2	2	2	2	2	2	1	2	2	2	2	2	2	2	2	2	2	2	1			42
Sergeants,	22	6	6	5	6	5	5	5	6	5	5	5	5	6	5	5	7	5	4	4	3			125
Patrolmen,	24	94	102	76	85	68	75	59	12	77	72	72	56	53	61	50	80	40	18	41	128			1,343
Clerks,	22																							22
Engineers,									3															3
Firemen,									7															7

TABLE I — *Concluded.*

RANK OR POSITION.	Headquarters	Div. 1	Div. 2	Div. 3	Div. 4	Div. 5	Div. 6	Div. 7	Div. 8	Div. 9	Div. 10	Div. 11	Div. 12	Div. 13	Div. 14	Div. 15	Div. 16	Div. 17	Div. 18	Div. 19	Traffic Police.	Signal Service.	House of Detention.	Totals.
Matrons (house of detention),	-	-	-	-	-	-	-	-	-	-	-	-	-	-	-	-	-	-	-	-	-	-	5	5
Matrons (stations),	-	-	-	-	-	-	1	1	-	1	1	-	-	1	-	1	-	-	-	1	-	-	-	7
Director, signal service,	-	-	-	-	-	-	-	-	-	-	-	-	-	-	-	-	-	-	-	-	-	1	-	1
Foreman,	-	-	-	-	-	-	-	-	-	-	-	-	-	-	-	-	-	-	-	-	-	1	-	1
Signalmen,	-	-	-	-	-	-	-	-	-	-	-	-	-	-	-	-	-	-	-	-	-	6	-	6
Mechanics,	-	-	-	-	-	-	-	-	-	-	-	-	-	-	-	-	-	-	-	-	-	3	-	3
Linemen,	-	-	-	-	-	-	-	-	-	-	-	-	-	-	-	-	-	-	-	-	-	6	-	6
Driver,	-	-	-	-	-	-	-	-	-	-	-	-	-	-	-	-	-	-	-	-	-	1	-	1
Van drivers,	-	-	-	-	-	-	-	-	-	-	-	-	-	-	-	-	-	-	-	-	-	-	2	2
Foreman of stable,	-	-	-	-	-	-	-	-	-	-	-	-	-	-	-	-	-	-	-	-	-	1	-	1
Hostlers,	-	-	-	-	-	-	-	-	-	-	-	-	-	-	-	-	5	-	-	-	-	4	-	9
Janitors,	1	2	1	2	2	2	1	-	1	1	1	-	-	1	-	-	1	1	-	-	-	-	-	17
Janitresses,	1	1	1	1	-	-	1	1	-	1	-	1	1	1	1	1	1	-	-	1	-	-	2	16
Assistant steward, city prison,	1	-	-	-	-	-	-	-	-	-	-	-	-	-	-	-	-	-	-	-	-	-	-	1
Telephone operators,	3	-	-	-	-	-	-	-	-	-	-	-	-	-	-	-	-	-	-	-	-	-	-	3
Totals,	116	106	113	86	96	79	86	69	31	89	83	81	65	65	70	60	97	49	26	50	132	23	9	1,681

TABLE II.

List of Police Officers in Active Service who died during the Year ending Nov. 30, 1919.

Rank.	Name.	Division.	Date of Death.	Cause of Death.
Patrolman,	John H. Bohling,	16	Apr. 29, 1919	Paralysis.
Patrolman,	Edward F. Brennan,	17	Feb. 2, 1919	Pleurisy.
Patrolman,	Adolph H. Butterman,	9	June 16, 1919	Bullet wound.
Patrolman,	Joseph F. Crotty,	9	Feb. 25, 1919	Fractured skull.
Patrolman,	Charles E. Deininger,	1	Feb. 13, 1919	Bullet wound.
Inspector,	Alfred N. Douglas,	B. C. I.	Apr. 26, 1919	Bright's disease.
Patrolman,	Michael M. Foley,	5	Apr. 8, 1919	Tuberculosis.
Patrolman,	Daniel J. Hart,	9	July 3, 1919	Heart disease.
Patrolman,	Thomas H. Hoadley,	12	June 29, 1919	Hemorrhage.
Patrolman,	Timothy W. Hurley,	3	Dec. 28, 1918	Pneumonia.
Lieutenant,	William J. Irwin,	5	Dec. 13, 1918	Pneumonia.

TABLE II — *Concluded.*

RANK.	NAME.	Division.	Date of Death.	Cause of Death.
Captain,	Hugh J. Lee,	9	May 2, 1919	Heart disease.
Lieutenant,	Albert F. Lovell,	9	July 7, 1919	Complication of diseases.
Patrolman,	Richard J. Lynch,	19	Sept. 22, 1919	Tuberculosis.
Inspector,	Thomas H. Lynch,	B. C. I.	Feb. 2, 1919	Pneumonia.
Patrolman,	Richard D. Reemts,	10	Sept. 11, 1919	Bullet wound.

TABLE III.

List of Officers retired during the Year, giving the Age at the Time of Retirement and the Number of Years' Service of Each.

NAME.	Cause of Retirement.	Age at Time of Retirement (Years).	Years of Service.
Bowers, Charles A.,	Incapacitated,	54	23
Burke, John H., [1]	Age,	74	22
Burr, Levi W.,	Age,	62	32
Colbert, James,	Age,	65	34
Duke, Patrick J.,	Incapacitated,	57	26
Hazlett, Henry,	Incapacitated,	53	30
Homer, Horatio J.,	Age,	71	40
Keenan, Thomas M.,	Incapacitated,	52	26
Mahoney, Jeremiah J., Jr.,	Incapacitated,	39	11
Merritt, Frank L.,	Incapacitated,	50	23
Morgan, Elam W.,	Incapacitated,	44	18
Orr, James S.,	Age,	64	34
Sanford, James E.,	Age,	63	37
Shaw, Thomas J.,	Age,	60	34
Weigel, John, [2]	Age,	72	31

[1] Employee in police signal service. [2] Director in police signal service.

TABLE IV.

List of Officers who were promoted above the Rank of Patrolman during the Year ending Nov. 30, 1919.

Date.	Name and Rank.
Jan. 31, 1919	Lieut. William L. Devitt to the rank of captain.
May 24, 1919	Lieut. Perley S. Skillings to the rank of captain.
Mar. 22, 1919	Sergt. Michael J. Burke to the rank of inspector.
Mar. 22, 1919	Sergt. James R. Claflin to the rank of inspector.
May 24, 1919	Sergt. James H. Eagan to the rank of inspector.
Mar. 22, 1919	Sergt. John F. Mitchell to the rank of inspector.
Mar. 22, 1919	Sergt. Patrick J. O'Neill to the rank of inspector.
Mar. 22, 1919	Sergt. Thomas M. Towle to the rank of inspector.
Mar. 22, 1919	Sergt. John F. Ahearn to the rank of lieutenant.
Sept. 15, 1919	Sergt. Frank Arnold to the rank of lieutenant.
Nov. 28, 1919	Sergt. Bernard J. Hoppe to the rank of lieutenant.
Sept. 15, 1919	Sergt. Mathew Killen to the rank of lieutenant.
Sept. 15, 1919	Sergt. Jeremiah J. Riordan to the rank of lieutenant.
Sept. 15, 1919	Sergt. Frank H. Thompson to the rank of lieutenant.
Mar. 29, 1919	Patrolman Benjamin Alexander to the rank of sergeant.
Mar. 29, 1919	Patrolman Delbert R. Augusta to the rank of sergeant.
Mar. 29, 1919	Patrolman Joseph W. Comerford to the rank of sergeant.
Mar. 29, 1919	Patrolman William F. Crawford to the rank of sergeant.
Mar. 29, 1919	Patrolman Timothy F. Donovan to the rank of sergeant.
Mar. 29, 1919	Patrolman John A. Dorsey to the rank of sergeant.
Mar. 29, 1919	Patrolman Frederick M. Finn to the rank of sergeant.
Mar. 29, 1919	Patrolman Stephen J. Flaherty to the rank of sergeant.
Mar. 29, 1919	Patrolman Francis P. Haggerty to the rank of sergeant.
Mar. 29, 1919	Patrolman Edward G. Kennedy to the rank of sergeant.
Mar. 29, 1919	Patrolman John F. McCarthy to the rank of sergeant.
Mar. 29, 1919	Patrolman Thomas F. Mulrey to the rank of sergeant.

TABLE V.

Number of Men in Active Service at the End of the Present Year who were appointed on the Force in the Year stated.

Date appointed.	Superintendent.	Deputy Superintendent.	Chief Inspector.	Captains.	Inspectors.	Lieutenants.	Sergeants.	Patrolmen.	Totals.
1869,	–	–	–	1	–	–	–	–	1
1875,	–	–	–	–	–	–	–	1	1
1878,	–	1	–	–	–	–	–	1	2
1879,	–	–	–	–	–	–	–	1	1
1880,	–	–	–	1	–	–	–	1	2
1881,	–	–	–	–	–	1	2	2	5
1882,	–	–	–	2	–	3	–	2	7
1883,	–	–	–	1	–	–	–	3	4
1884,	–	–	–	–	–	–	–	5	5
1885,	–	–	–	1	1	1	1	7	11
1886,	–	–	–	3	1	–	–	6	10
1887,	–	–	–	–	3	2	1	12	18
1888,	1	–	–	2	1	6	2	25	37
1889,	–	–	–	1	2	–	1	10	14
1890,	–	–	–	1	2	2	4	9	18
1891,	–	–	1	2	–	1	2	8	14
1892,	–	–	–	1	1	3	2	10	17
1893,	–	–	–	3	4	6	12	31	56
1894,	–	–	–	2	–	1	6	8	17
1895,	–	–	–	4	4	7	18	54	87
1896,	–	–	–	–	2	1	1	9	13
1897,	–	–	–	–	1	–	2	5	8
1898,	–	–	–	–	–	2	4	16	22
1900,	–	–	–	1	3	2	16	33	55
1901,	–	–	–	–	1	1	10	9	21
1902,	–	–	–	–	–	–	1	1	2
1903,	–	–	–	–	–	2	7	25	34
1904,	–	–	–	–	1	–	5	18	24
1905,	–	–	–	–	–	–	5	5	10
1906,	–	–	–	–	–	–	4	5	9
1907,	–	–	–	–	–	–	8	16	24
1908,	–	–	–	–	–	–	6	18	24
1909,	–	–	–	–	–	–	3	6	9
1910,	–	–	–	–	1	–	2	5	8
1911,	–	–	–	–	–	–	–	5	5
1912,	–	–	–	1	–	1	–	13	15
1913,	–	–	–	–	–	–	–	3	3
1914,	–	–	–	–	–	–	–	2	2
1915,	–	–	–	–	–	–	–	3	3
1916,	–	–	–	–	–	–	–	3	3
1917,	–	–	–	–	–	–	–	8	8
1918,	–	–	–	–	–	–	–	2	2
1919,	–	–	–	–	–	–	–	937	937
Totals,	1	1	1	27	28	42	125	1,343	1,568

TABLE VI.

Officers discharged and resigned during the Year ending Nov. 30, 1919.

Rank.	Name.	Discharged.	Resigned.	Length of Service.
Patrolman,	Richard J. Austin,	Sept. 13, 1919	—	13½12 years.
Patrolman,	Joseph J. Barry,	—	Nov. 27, 1919	1 day.
Patrolman,	Jesse E. Boothby,	—	Dec. 22, 1918	3⁹⁄12 years.
Patrolman,	William F. Brown,	Sept. 13, 1919	—	6³⁄12 years.
Patrolman,	Edmund J. Burke,	Sept. 13, 1919	—	13½12 years.
Patrolman,	James L. Butler,	Sept. 13, 1919	—	10¹¹⁄12 years.
Patrolman,	William E. Clouten,	Nov. 26, 1919	—	⁷⁄12 year.
Patrolman,	Philip S. Corbett,	Sept. 13, 1919	—	4⁶⁄12 years.
Patrolman,	Henry T. Cunniff,	Jan. 25, 1919	—	5⁵⁄12 years.
Patrolman,	John F. Cunningham,	Oct. 29, 1919	—	14 days.
Patrolman,	James F. Dillon,	Nov. 22, 1919	—	14 days.
Patrolman,	John F. Dolan,	May 5, 1919	—	10⁵⁄12 years.
Patrolman,	John J. Driscoll,	—	Aug. 13, 1919	1 month.
Patrolman,	Thomas J. Driscoll,	Sept. 13, 1919	—	3⁴⁄12 years.
Patrolman,	Stephen J. Dunleavy,	Sept. 13, 1919	—	8½12 years.
Patrolman,	John H. Falvey,	—	May 9, 1919	1 year.
Patrolman,	George E. Ferreira,	Sept. 13, 1919	—	1¹⁰⁄12 years.
Reserve man,	Morris C. Fouhy,	—	Dec. 9, 1918	⁷⁄12 year.
Patrolman,	William J. Gallagher,	May 21, 1919	—	5¹¹⁄12 years.
Patrolman,	Hugh H. Garrity,	Sept. 13, 1919	—	7¹⁰⁄12 years.
Patrolman,	James J. Garrity,	Sept. 13, 1919	—	8⁶⁄12 years.
Patrolman,	James C. Good,	Nov. 6, 1919	—	8 days.

Rank	Name			
Patrolman,	Daniel E. Grant,	–	Feb. 4, 1919	13 4/12 years.
Patrolman,	Herbert T. Greeley,	–	Aug. 19, 1919	2 6/12 years.
Patrolman,	Robert S. Greene,	Apr. 17, 1919	–	1 1/12 years.
Reserve man,	Charles E. Guittarr,	–	Dec. 2, 1918	5 days.
Patrolman,	Archie E. Hamlet,	–	Mar. 19, 1919	4/12 year.
Patrolman,	James J. Hart,	–	Jan. 9, 1919	6 11/12 years.
Patrolman,	John Hourihan,	–	Aug. 13, 1919	1/12 year.
Patrolman,	Joseph L. Howe,	–	Mar. 10, 1919	2 years.
Patrolman,	Michael J. Joyce,	Sept. 13, 1919	–	1 7/12 years.
Patrolman,	John P. Kane,	–	Oct. 17, 1919	2 days.
Patrolman,	William J. Kane,	Sept. 13, 1919	Oct. 3, 1919	1 day.
Patrolman,	Michael L. King,	Dec. 9, 1918	–	13 4/12 years.
Patrolman,	William T. Kirley,	–	–	23 7/12 years.
Patrolman,	Grover E. Ladd,	–	Nov. 19, 1919	1/12 year.
Patrolman,	Oscar J. Lavoie,	–	Nov. 3, 1919	6 days.
Patrolman,	William R. Leary,	–	May 22, 1919	11 1/12 years.
Patrolman,	John F. Leavitt,	–	Nov. 25, 1919	27 days.
Patrolman,	Daniel J. Lee,	Feb. 13, 1919	–	1 2/12 years.
Patrolman,	Daniel J. Lynch,	May 13, 1919	–	16 1/12 years.
Patrolman,	Eugene F. Lynch,	Nov. 6, 1919	–	29 days.
Patrolman,	William L. Malone,	Oct. 29, 1919	–	6 days.
Patrolman,	John J. Maloney,	Sept. 13, 1919	–	1 1/12 year.
Patrolman,	Frank H. Mealey,	Nov. 6, 1919	–	6 days.
Patrolman,	Edward J. Merrigan,	–	July 7, 1919	1 day.
Patrolman,	James T. Monahan,	–	Dec. 31, 1918	13 5/12 years.
Patrolman,	Edmond Morrison,	Mar. 6, 1919	–	8 years.
Patrolman,	Grover W. Mullen,	Jan. 21, 1919	–	5 5/12 years.

Table VI — *Concluded.*

Rank.	Name.	Discharged.	Resigned.	Length of Service.
Patrolman,	Martin F. Mullen,	Apr. 17, 1919	—	$16\frac{1}{12}$ years.
Patrolman,	John J. Murray,	Apr. 17, 1919	—	$1\frac{4}{12}$ years.
Patrolman,	Joseph A. McCulloch,	—	Aug. 6, 1919	$\frac{7}{12}$ year.
Patrolman,	John J. McGowan,	—	Oct. 2, 1919	1 day.
Patrolman,	John F. McInnes,	Sept. 13, 1919	—	$11\frac{11}{12}$ years.
Patrolman,	Mack McKenzie,	—	Nov. 29, 1919	$\frac{1}{12}$ year.
Patrolman,	William E. Nolan,	—	Jan. 31, 1919	$2\frac{8}{12}$ years.
Patrolman,	Richard T. O'Brien,	—	Nov. 10, 1919	3 days.
Patrolman,	John C. O'Connor,	—	Jan. 28, 1919	$2\frac{8}{12}$ years.
Patrolman,	John H. O'Hare,	Sept. 13, 1919	—	$9\frac{6}{12}$ years.
Patrolman,	Thomas H. O'Neil,	—	Nov. 10, 1919	14 days.
Patrolman,	James G. Peters,	Sept. 13, 1919	—	$13\frac{1}{12}$ years.
Patrolman,	Nicholas H. Prempas,	—	Dec. 13, 1918	$6\frac{4}{12}$ years.
Patrolman,	Harry Quirk,	Jan. 30, 1919	—	$15\frac{5}{12}$ years.
Patrolman,	James Rafferty,	—	May 3, 1919	$7\frac{3}{12}$ years.
Patrolman,	Patrick Raftery,	—	Aug. 5, 1919	$1\frac{9}{12}$ year.
Patrolman,	Thomas F. Robinson,	—	Oct. 17, 1919	1 day.
Patrolman,	Stephen J. Ryder,	Sept. 13, 1919	—	$4\frac{9}{12}$ years.
Patrolman,	Gustave A. Sandberg,	—	Feb. 19, 1919	$11\frac{1}{12}$ years.
Patrolman,	Anthony B. Schlenkert,	—	Mar. 25, 1919	$2\frac{11}{12}$ years.
Patrolman,	John J. Sheehan,	—	Mar. 8, 1919	$\frac{5}{12}$ year.
Patrolman,	William M. Sheehan,	Nov. 4, 1919	—	12 days.
Patrolman,	Francis A. Slater,	—	Dec. 5, 1918	$2\frac{11}{12}$ years.

Patrolman,	Clifford E. Smith,	—	Jan. 1, 1919	15 10/12 years.
Patrolman,	Michael Sperouffske,	—	Nov. 5, 1919	20 days.
Patrolman,	Walter F. Spratt,	—	Mar. 24, 1919	3/12 year.
Patrolman,	John L. Sullivan,	—	July 8, 1919	5 1/12 years.
Patrolman,	Philip A. Sullivan,	—	Oct. 3, 1919	1 day.
Patrolman,	Joseph B. Swanson,	—	Jan. 27, 1919	5 11/12 years.
Patrolman,	James J. Tansey,	—	Nov. 25, 1919	2/12 year.
Patrolman,	William R. Thompson,	Oct. 6, 1919	—	4 days.
Patrolman,	John H. Webber,	—	Nov. 17, 1919	5 days.
Patrolman,	John F. Welch,	—	Oct. 29, 1919	14 days.
Patrolman,	John P. Whitten,	Sept. 13, 1919	—	9 5/12 years.
Patrolman,	William P. Wills,	Sept. 13, 1919	—	15 7/12 years.
Patrolman,	Herbert L. Wingate,	—	June 26, 1919	18 10/12 years.
Patrolman,	Albert Wood,	Nov. 6, 1919	—	22 days.

TABLE VII.

Number of Days' Absence from Duty by Reason of Sickness during the Year ending Nov. 30, 1919.

	Reserve.	Regular.		Reserve.	Regular.
December, 1918,[1]	81	1,110	July, 1919,	—	707
January, 1919,[1]	105	1,518	August, 1919,	—	793
February, 1919,[1]	53	1,091	September, 1919,	—	1,093
March, 1919,	—	1,106	October, 1919,	—	630
April, 1919,	—	1,162	November, 1919,	—	522
May, 1919,	—	967			
June, 1919,	—	734	Totals,	239	11,433

Average number of men on the force, ... reserve, 19; regular, 1,548.

Average number of sick daily, including reserve men, ... 32, or 2.18 per cent.

[1] The rank of reserve man was abolished by statute on Feb. 19, 1919.

TABLE VIII.

Complaints against Officers during the Year ending Nov. 30, 1919.

No.	Rank.	Nature of Complaint.	Disposition of Case.
27	Patrolman, .	Joining and belonging to an organization outside of the police department in violation of section 19 of Rule 35 of the Department Rules.	Guilty; dismissed from police force.
8	Patrolman, .	Neglect of duty, ...	Guilty; dismissed from police force.
2	Patrolman, .	Intoxication, ...	Guilty; dismissed from police force.
1	Patrolman, .	Engaging in private business, . . .	Guilty; dismissed from police force.
2	Patrolman, .	Conduct unbecoming an officer, . . .	Guilty; dismissed from police force.
2	Patrolman, .	Not patrolling or not properly patrolling route during tour of patrol duty.	Guilty; dismissed from police force.
4	Patrolman, .	Neglect of duty, ...	Guilty; sentenced to perform 210 hours' punishment duty.
1	Patrolman, .	Not patrolling or not properly patrolling route during tour of patrol duty.	Guilty; sentenced to perform 210 hours' punishment duty.
1	Patrolman, .	Engaging in private business, . . .	Guilty; sentenced to perform 170 hours' punishment duty.

TABLE VIII — *Concluded.*

No.	Rank.	Nature of Complaint.	Disposition of Case.
1	Patrolman,	Neglect of duty,	Guilty; sentenced to perform 140 hours' punishment duty.
1	Patrolman,	Not being punctual in attendance at court,	Guilty; sentenced to perform 105 hours' punishment duty.
1	Patrolman,	Neglect of duty,	Guilty; sentenced to perform 90 hours' punishment duty.
1	Patrolman,	Neglect of duty,	Guilty; sentenced to perform 70 hours' punishment duty.
6	Patrolman,	Neglect of duty,	Resigned, pending charges.
2	Patrolman,	Conduct unbecoming an officer,	Resigned, pending charges.
1	Patrolman,	Engaging in private business,	Resigned, pending charges.
2	Sergeant,	Failure to report officer's absence from route,	Reprimanded in General Orders.
13	Patrolman,	Joining and belonging to an organization outside of the police department in violation of section 19 of Rule 35 of the Department Rules, and absence without leave.	Sentence suspended.
13	Patrolman,	Joining and belonging to an organization outside of the police department in violation of section 19 of Rule 35 of the Department Rules.	Sentence suspended.

1	Patrolman,	Absence without leave,	Sentence suspended.
1	Patrolman,	Neglect of duty,	On account of defendant abandoning position the hearing was cancelled.
1	Patrolman,	Joining and belonging to an organization outside of the police department in violation of section 19 of Rule 35 of the Department Rules.	On account of defendant abandoning position the hearing was cancelled.
1	Patrolman,	Neglect of duty,	Complaint dismissed.
1	Patrolman,	Absence without leave,	Complaint dismissed.
2	Patrolman,	Joining and belonging to an organization outside of the police department in violation of section 19 of Rule 35 of the Department Rules.	Complaint dismissed.
1	Patrolman,	Neglect of duty,	Complaint placed on file.
1	Patrolman,	Absence without leave,	Complaint placed on file.
1	Patrolman,	Joining and belonging to an organization outside of the police department in violation of section 19 of Rule 35 of the Department Rules.	Complaint placed on file.

TABLE IX.

Number and Distribution of Horses used in Department.

DIVISIONS.	Wagons.	Vans.	Patrol.	Riding.	Ambulance.	Driving.	Totals.
Division 1, ...	–	–	–	–	1	–	1
Division 16, . . .	–	–	–	16	–	–	16
Signal service repair department, 40 Joy Street.	3	–	1	5	–	1	10
Prison van, ...	–	4	–	–	–	–	4
Totals, ...	3	4	1	21	1	1	31

TABLE X.

Number of Arrests by Police Divisions during the Year ending Nov. 30, 1919.

DIVISIONS.	Males.	Females.	Totals.
Headquarters, ...	1,152	426	1,578
Division 1, ...	8,079	492	8,571
Division 2, ...	4,575	592	5,167
Division 3, ...	11,019	1,115	12,134
Division 4, ...	5,914	426	6,340
Division 5, ...	5,214	953	6,167
Division 6, ...	3,025	169	3,194
Division 7, ...	2,563	160	2,723
Division 8, ...	19	1	20
Division 9, ...	3,745	250	3,995
Division 10, ...	3,772	355	4,127
Division 11, ...	2,155	68	2,223
Division 12, ...	1,044	48	1,092
Division 13, ...	851	34	885
Division 14, ...	1,153	84	1,237
Division 15, ...	2,861	194	3,055
Division 16, ...	3,055	222	3,277
Division 17, ...	955	18	973
Division 18, ...	345	14	359
Division 19, ...	788	42	830
Totals, ...	62,284	5,663	67,947

TABLE XI.

Arrests and Offences for Year ending Nov. 30, 1919.

No. 1. OFFENCES AGAINST THE PERSON.

NATURE OF OFFENCE.	Sex. Males.	Sex. Females.	Total.	On Warrants.	Without Warrants.	Summoned by the Court.	Foreigners.	Non-residents.	Minors.	Held for Trial.	Discharged or to United States Authorities.
Affray, engaging in,	38	2	40	6	28	6	17	20	12	40	—
Assault,	67	1	68	28	29	11	36	7	12	68	—
Assault and battery,	1,474	202	1,676	726	484	466	873	236	225	1,676	—
Assault, felonious,	18	—	18	11	7	—	11	4	3	18	—
Assault, indecent,	32	—	32	14	17	1	14	3	7	32	—
Assault on police,	87	2	89	45	41	3	19	21	22	89	—
Blackmailing,	1	—	1	—	1	—	—	—	—	1	—
Child, abandoning,	1	2	3	3	—	—	1	—	—	3	—
Child, female, abuse of,	23	2	25	19	6	—	20	2	2	25	—
Child, refusing to support,	65	5	70	65	—	5	35	5	4	70	—
Children, minor, neglecting,	3	7	10	6	—	4	2	2	1	10	—
Extortion, or attempt,	3	—	3	2	1	—	2	—	2	3	—

Family, abandoning or neglecting,	52	6	58	57	—	1	15	8	2	58	—
Family, refusing to support,	710	2	712	641	8	63	301	95	20	712	—
Illegitimate child, refusing to support,	1	—	1	1	—	—	1	—	—	1	—
Intimidation and threatening language, using,	82	4	86	71	1	14	61	5	1	86	—
Kidnapping,	—	3	3	3	—	—	2	1	—	3	—
Manslaughter,	82	1	83	21	61	1	27	27	12	83	—
Mayhem,	1	—	1	—	1	—	—	1	—	1	—
Murder,	20	4	24	14	10	—	14	4	3	24	—
Murder, accessory to,	2	1	3	3	—	—	—	1	—	3	—
Murder, assault with intent to,	74	3	77	32	45	—	51	13	3	77	—
Parent law, violation of,	29	8	37	14	—	23	17	10	2	37	—
Rape,	24	—	24	19	5	—	13	3	4	24	—
Rape, assault to,	11	—	11	8	3	—	8	1	1	11	—
Riot, or inciting to,	88	14	102	6	96	—	85	47	7	102	—
Rob, assault to,	51	—	51	29	21	1	5	12	12	51	—
Robbery,	232	3	235	107	126	2	55	62	52	235	—
Sodomy and other unnatural practices,	8	—	8	5	3	—	1	2	1	8	—
Totals,	3,279	272	3,551	1,956	994	601	1,686	592	410	3,551	—

TABLE XI — *Continued.*

No. 2. OFFENCES AGAINST PROPERTY, COMMITTED WITH VIOLENCE.

NATURE OF OFFENCE.	Sex. Males.	Sex. Females.	Total.	On Warrants.	Without Warrants.	Summoned by the Court.	Foreigners.	Non-residents.	Minors.	Held for Trial.	Discharged or to United States Authorities.
Breaking and entering dwelling at night,	90	3	93	49	44	–	24	19	32	93	–
Breaking and entering dwelling at night, attempted.	1	–	1	–	1	–	1	–	–	1	–
Breaking and entering dwelling by day,	100	11	111	59	51	1	31	24	32	111	–
Breaking and entering dwelling by day, attempted.	6	2	8	5	2	1	3	3	1	8	–
Breaking and entering a building,	445	4	449	153	289	7	66	74	223	449	–
Breaking and entering a building, attempted.	28	–	28	3	25	–	2	5	14	28	–
Breaking and entering vessels,	5	–	5	1	4	–	1	–	4	5	–
Breaking and entering railroad car,	18	–	18	5	13	–	–	–	7	18	–
Breaking and entering railroad car, attempted.	2	–	2	1	1	–	–	–	2	2	–
Tree, injury to,	1	–	1	–	–	1	1	–	–	1	–
Totals,	696	20	716	276	430	10	129	125	315	716	–

No. 3. Offences against Property, committed without Violence.

Animals, vehicles and boats, using without consent of owner.	71	—	71	38	16	17	6	7	41	71	—
Automobile, unlawful appropriation,	4	—	4	1	3	—	—	1	2	4	—
Buildings, defacing, etc.,	1	—	1	—	—	1	1	1	—	1	—
Burglar's tools, having in possession,	13	—	13	13	1	—	1	2	2	13	—
Conspiring to defraud,	43	—	43	42	8	—	9	6	1	43	—
Innholders, boarding-house keepers, etc., defrauding.	22	3	25	17	1	—	7	17	10	25	—
Lamps, extinguishing, breaking, etc.,	6	—	6	5	1	—	3	1	—	6	—
Larceny,	2,325	792	3,117	1,150	1,810	157	1,003	1,012	738	3,117	—
Larceny, accessory after fact,	1	—	1	—	1	—	—	—	—	1	—
Larceny in building, attempt to commit,	1	—	1	—	1	—	—	1	1	1	—
Larceny from person,	178	24	202	59	139	4	59	52	41	202	—
Larceny from person, attempt to commit,	54	4	58	8	48	2	19	18	11	58	—
Larceny, attempt to commit,	59	2	61	25	36	—	14	20	19	61	—
Larceny in a building or vessel,	10	1	11	8	3	—	1	1	5	11	—
Larceny from an express,	25	—	25	7	18	—	4	5	7	25	—
Larceny from realty,	6	—	6	—	2	4	—	1	4	6	—
Leased property, concealing, conveying, selling, etc.	26	6	32	30	—	2	13	7	2	32	—

TABLE XI — *Continued.*

No. 3. OFFENCES AGAINST PROPERTY, COMMITTED WITHOUT VIOLENCE — *Concluded.*

NATURE OF OFFENCE.	SEX.		Total.	On Warrants.	Without Warrants.	Summoned by the Court.	Foreigners.	Non-residents.	Minors.	Held for Trial.	Discharged or to United States Authorities.
	Males.	Females.									
Mortgaged property, concealing, conveying, selling, etc.	8	–	8	7	–	1	6	2	–	8	–
Stolen goods, buying, receiving, etc.,	245	26	271	152	91	28	155	51	35	271	–
Taxi-cab fare, evading,	1	1	2	2	–	–	–	2	1	2	–
Trespass,	341	11	352	20	269	63	130	82	123	352	–
Totals,	3,440	870	4,310	1,584	2,447	279	1,431	1,289	1,043	4,310	–

No. 4. MALICIOUS OFFENCES AGAINST PROPERTY.

NATURE OF OFFENCE.	SEX.		Total.	On Warrants.	Without Warrants.	Summoned by the Court.	Foreigners.	Non-residents.	Minors.	Held for Trial.	Discharged or to United States Authorities.
	Males.	Females.									
Arson and other burnings,	3	–	3	–	3	–	–	1	1	3	–
Malicious mischief,	87	10	97	49	27	21	37	18	22	97	–
Slot-machine, wilfully breaking,	6	–	6	–	–	6	1	–	6	6	–
Wilful damage and trespass,	37	3	40	27	3	10	7	3	16	40	–
Totals,	133	13	146	76	33	37	45	22	45	146	–

No. 5. FORGERY AND OFFENCES AGAINST THE CURRENCY.

Counterfeit money, passing, etc.,	2	–	2	–	2	–	2	1	1	2	–
Forgery and uttering,	79	7	86	63	23	–	17	36	19	86	–
Worthless check, passing,	1	–	1	1	–	–	–	–	–	1	–
Totals,	82	7	89	64	25	–	19	37	20	89	–

No. 6. OFFENCES AGAINST THE LICENSE LAWS.

Auctioneer's license law, violation of,	2	–	2	–	2	1	–	–	2	–
Carriage regulations, violation of,	4	–	4	–	4	2	1	–	4	–
Common victualler and innholder, assuming to be,	5	–	5	1	4	4	–	1	5	–
Dentist, practicing unlawfully,	1	–	1	1	–	1	–	–	1	–
Dog law, violation of,	23	3	26	–	26	14	–	3	26	–
Insurance broker, assuming to be,	1	–	1	1	–	–	–	–	1	–
Intelligence office, keeping unlawfully,	3	1	4	–	4	3	1	–	4	–
Junk, dealing in unlawfully,	9	1	10	3	6	8	3	1	10	–
Liquor law, violation of,	169	23	192	102	24	121	19	6	192	–
Lodging house law, violation of,	54	57	111	50	54	60	13	9	111	–

TABLE XI — *Continued.*

No. 6. OFFENCES AGAINST THE LICENSE LAWS — *Concluded.*

NATURE OF OFFENCE.	Sex.		Total.	On Warrants.	Without Warrants.	Summoned by the Court.	Foreigners.	Non-residents.	Minors.	Held for Trial.	Discharged or to United States Authorities.
	Males.	Females.									
Lying-in hospital law, violation of,	1	—	1	1	—	—	—	—	—	1	—
Merchandise, sale or storage of, in public place.	257	3	260	2	148	110	225	11	20	260	—
Milk law, violation of,	37	1	38	—	—	38	16	5	—	38	—
Pawnbroker, assuming to be,	1	—	1	—	—	1	1	—	—	1	—
Peddling without a license,	44	—	44	1	38	5	33	7	16	44	—
Peddler's license law, violation of,	1	—	1	1	—	—	1	—	1	1	—
Physician, practicing unlawfully,	7	2	9	7	—	2	6	—	1	9	—
Pool and billiard room, unlawfully admitting minor to.	3	—	3	—	—	3	1	—	—	3	—
Public amusement, unlawfully maintaining,	5	2	7	—	—	7	—	—	1	7	—
Revolver, carrying without license,	19	—	19	6	11	2	11	2	5	19	—
Second-hand articles, dealing in unlawfully.	11	—	11	2	—	9	9	1	1	11	—
United States liquor law, violation of,	1	—	1	1	—	—	1	—	—	1	—
Totals,	658	93	751	179	271	301	518	63	63	751	—

No. 7. Offences against Chastity, Morality, etc.

Abortion,	6	3	9	8	1	–	4	–	–	9	–	–
Abortion instruments, having in possession.	1	1	2	2	–	–	2	–	–	2	–	–
Abduction,	3	–	3	1	2	–	3	1	–	3	–	–
Adultery,	80	68	148	35	111	2	54	30	8	148	–	–
Animals, cruelty to,	30	1	31	5	6	20	15	6	3	31	–	–
Bastardy,	93	–	93	89	1	3	27	29	19	93	–	–
Bigamy,	2	1	3	3	–	–	2	1	–	3	–	–
Conception, instruments to prevent, having for sale or in possession.	2	–	2	1	–	1	–	–	–	2	–	–
Disorderly house, keeping,	1	–	1	1	–	–	–	–	–	1	–	–
Female, annoying or accosting with offensive language.	47	1	48	16	28	4	24	12	4	48	–	–
Female under eighteen years, inducing to have sexual intercourse.	1	–	1	1	–	–	1	–	–	1	–	–
Fornication,	415	420	835	29	806	–	233	261	52	835	–	–
Illegitimate child law, violation of,	34	–	34	29	–	5	8	7	4	34	–	–
Ill-fame, keeping house of,	19	19	38	29	9	–	16	1	–	38	–	–
Incest,	1	–	1	1	–	–	–	–	1	1	–	–
Indecent exposure of the person,	42	1	43	6	37	–	13	5	3	43	–	–

TABLE XI — *Continued.*

No. 7. OFFENCES AGAINST CHASTITY, MORALITY, ETC. — *Concluded.*

NATURE OF OFFENCE.	SEX.		Total.	On Warrants.	Without Warrants.	Summoned by the Court.	Foreigners.	Non-residents.	Minors.	Held for Trial.	Discharged or to United States Authorities.
	Males.	Females.									
Lewd and lascivious cohabitation,	160	163	323	92	228	3	103	25	24	323	–
Lewd person, in speech and behavior,	3	4	7	1	6	–	1	3	3	7	–
Night walking,	–	68	68	3	65	–	21	15	21	68	–
Obscene books and prints,	20	–	20	16	4	–	12	6	1	20	–
Open and gross lewdness,	8	2	10	5	4	1	5	2	3	10	–
Polygamy,	9	2	11	11	–	–	7	3	–	11	–
Prostitute, deriving support from,	4	–	4	3	1	–	3	1	–	4	–
Prostitution, enticing to,	2	1	3	2	1	–	2	–	–	3	–
Public conveyance, being disorderly in,	8	–	8	5	2	1	1	5	1	8	–
School, disturbing,	3	–	3	–	–	3	–	–	3	3	–
Unnatural and lascivious acts,	13	1	14	7	7	–	–	6	1	14	–
Totals,	1,007	756	1,763	401	1,319	43	557	419	151	1,763	–

No. 8. OFFENCES NOT INCLUDED IN THE FOREGOING.

Offence											
Adulterating food, drugs, butter, etc.,	127	1	128	3	3	122	42	60	11	128	—
Agricultural law, violation of,	1	–	1	–	–	1	–	–	–	1	—
Air rifle, selling to minor,	1	–	1	1	–	–	–	1	1	1	—
Alms, soliciting,	1	–	1	1	–	–	–	–	–	1	—
Anti-anarchy law, violation of,	5	2	7	4	3	–	4	3	–	7	—
Automobile law, violation of,	5,562	36	5,598	279	240	5,079	1,146	2,926	683	5,598	—
Bail bond,	6	–	6	2	4	–	2	–	–	6	—
Bets, registering,	6	–	6	3	3	–	1	5	2	6	—
Bicycle, riding on sidewalk,	2	–	2	–	1	1	2	2	–	2	—
Bonfire, making,	1	–	1	–	1	–	1	–	–	1	—
Bribery,	1	–	1	–	1	–	–	–	–	1	—
Bucket shop, keeping,	2	–	2	2	–	–	–	2	–	2	—
Business, doing under assumed name,	1	–	1	–	–	1	–	–	–	1	—
Capias,	85	7	92	49	17	26	26	9	54	92	—
Children, delinquent,	2,914	147	3,061	286	1,192	1,583	354	182	3,061	3,061	—
Children, neglected,	93	82	175	166	4	5	8	3	175	175	—
Children, wayward,	8	12	20	8	11	1	1	5	19	20	—

TABLE XI—*Continued.*

No. 8. OFFENCES NOT INCLUDED IN THE FOREGOING—*Continued.*

NATURE OF OFFENCE.	Sex.		Total.	On Warrants.	Without Warrants.	Summoned by the Court.	Foreigners.	Non-residents.	Minors.	Held for Trial.	Discharged or to United States Authorities.
	Males.	Females.									
City ordinance, violation of,	482	43	525	75	243	207	157	74	196	525	—
Cocaine law, violation of,	6	2	8	5	3	—	1	2	—	8	—
Common nuisance, keeping,	24	16	40	31	8	1	21	1	2	40	—
Common brawlers,	—	9	9	1	—	8	5	—	—	9	—
Concealed weapons, carrying,	213	7	220	79	140	1	106	61	45	220	—
Contempt of court,	3	1	4	2	1	1	3	—	—	4	—
Crime, soliciting person to commit,	1	—	1	1	—	—	1	—	—	1	—
Dazzling light law, violation of,	2	—	2	—	—	2	1	1	1	2	—
Dagger, carrying,	1	—	1	—	1	—	1	—	—	1	—
Default warrant,	374	61	435	434	1	—	146	93	87	435	—
Delinquent law, violation of,	—	1	1	—	—	1	—	—	—	1	—
Denatured alcohol, unlawful sale of,	1	—	1	—	—	1	—	—	—	1	—
Deserters,	105	—	105	2	103	—	20	44	32	—	105
Disorderly,	341	91	432	—	432	—	98	188	160	—	432

Offense											
District Police rules, violation of,	3	–	3	–	–	3	–	–	–	–	3
Disturbing the peace,	82	13	95	20	36	39	25	8	51	95	–
Drunkard, common,	7	2	9	8	–	1	1	–	–	9	–
Drunkenness,	33,040	2,500	35,540	38	35,502	–	14,424	18,124	480	35,540	–
Election law, violation of,	3	–	3	–	3	–	–	1	–	3	–
Eavesdropping,	1	–	1	–	1	–	–	.1	–	1	–
Electrician, unlicensed,	1	–	1	–	–	1	1	–	–	1	–
Electricity, unlawfully diverting,	1	–	1	–	–	1	1	–	–	1	–
Expectoration law, violation of,	457	–	457	19	263	175	271	123	43	457	–
Federal law, violation of,	2	–	2	–	2	–	2	–	–	–	2
Fire alarm, giving false or tampering with,	11	–	11	2	9	–	2	–	6	11	–
Firearms, selling to minor,	1	–	1	–	–	1	1	–	–	1	–
Fire Commissioner's rules, violation of,	2	–	2	–	–	2	–	–	1	2	–
Fire prevention rules, violation of,	4	–	4	2	–	2	2	1	–	4	–
Fire escape, obstructing,	3	3	6	1	–	5	6	–	–	6	–
Fugitive from justice,	61	5	66	44	22	–	20	35	9	66	–
Gaming and being present at,	512	–	512	79	43	390	233	75	124	512	–
Gaming house, keeping,	14	–	14	14	–	–	8	2	–	14	–

TABLE XI — *Continued.*

No. 8. OFFENCES NOT INCLUDED IN THE FOREGOING — *Continued.*

NATURE OF OFFENCE.	SEX.		Total.	On Warrants.	Without Warrants.	Summoned by the Court.	Foreigners.	Non-residents.	Minors.	Held for Trial.	Discharged or to United States Authorities.
	Males.	Females.									
Gaming implements, being present where found.	497	–	497	120	377	–	385	60	17	497	–
Gaming on the Lord's Day and being present at.	1,486	2	1,488	57	1,335	96	754	103	441	1,488	–
Glass, maliciously breaking.	33	2	35	21	7	7	–	8	13	35	–
Health law, violation of.	19	–	19	11	–	8	14	4	2	19	–
Highway Commission regulations, violation of.	1	–	1	1	–	–	–	–	–	1	–
Hypnotic law, violation of.	65	16	81	33	47	1	16	13	4	81	–
Idle and disorderly persons.	95	148	243	99	144	–	62	50	81	243	–
Immigration law, violation of.	1	1	2	2	–	–	2	1	1	–	2
Inebriety.	1	–	1	1	–	–	–	–	–	1	1
Income tax law, violation of.	2	–	2	2	–	–	2	2	–	–	2
Insane person.	1	–	1	1	–	–	1	–	–	1	1
Interstate commerce act, violation of.	5	–	5	5	–	–	3	3	–	–	5
Internal revenue act, violation of.	2	–	2	–	2	–	2	–	–	–	2
Jewelry peddling.	3	–	3	1	2	–	2	1	–	3	–

Justice, obstructing,	-	2	-	1	-	-	-	2	2	-	2
Labels, counterfeiting,	-	1	-	1	1	1	-	-	1	-	1
Labor law, violation of,	-	8	-	-	5	7	-	1	8	-	8
Legal business, soliciting,	-	1	-	-	-	-	-	1	1	-	1
Liquor, giving or selling to soldiers and sailors in uniform.	131	-	8	53	29	-	130	1	131	2	129
Loitering in South Station,	-	1	-	-	-	-	1	-	1	-	1
Lotteries and prize enterprises,	-	62	3	14	41	-	42	20	62	-	62
Masked ball, promoting,	-	2	-	-	2	-	-	2	2	-	2
Militia law, violation of,	-	15	1	3	1	7	5	3	15	-	15
Minor child labor law, violation of,	-	8	-	-	5	8	-	-	8	-	8
Minor child parent law, violation of,	1	1	-	-	-	1	-	-	1	-	1
Military law, violation of (not wearing uniform).	1	-	-	-	-	-	1	-	1	1	1
Missiles, throwing in public streets,	-	1	1	-	1	-	1	-	1	-	1
Morphine law, violation of,	4	44	1	6	8	-	35	9	44	14	30
Naval prisoners, escaped,	-	-	2	-	-	-	4	-	4	-	4
Noisy and disorderly house, keeping,	-	16	-	-	7	1	1	14	16	9	7
Officer, assuming to be,	-	5	-	-	1	-	1	4	5	-	5
Officer, refusing to assist,	-	2	-	-	1	-	-	2	2	-	2

Table XI — *Continued.*

No. 8. Offences not included in the Foregoing — *Continued.*

NATURE OF OFFENCE.	Sex.		Total.	On Warrants.	Without Warrants.	Summoned by the Court.	Foreigners.	Non-residents.	Minors.	Held for Trial.	Discharged or to United States Authorities.
	Males.	Females.									
Opium law, violation of,	39	–	39	–	39	–	39	8	1	39	–
Pardon, violation of conditions,	1	–	1	1	–	–	–	–	–	–	1
Parole, violation of conditions,	40	6	46	29	17	–	8	6	24	45	1
Perjury, and subornation of,	9	4	13	11	2	–	2	2	1	13	–
Plumbing law, violation of,	2	–	2	1	–	1	1	1	–	2	–
Police rules, violation of,	42	–	42	4	5	33	19	7	2	42	–
Postal law, violation of,	1	–	1	1	–	–	1	–	–	1	–
Prisoner, escaped,	16	2	18	3	15	–	2	6	6	16	2
Prisoner, aiding to escape,	1	2	3	3	–	–	–	1	–	3	–
Prisoner, rescue or attempt to rescue,	41	1	42	15	27	–	11	10	6	42	–
Probation, violation of conditions,	215	43	258	245	13	–	82	18	75	258	–
Provost guard, interfering with,	2	–	2	–	2	–	–	–	–	2	–
Public meetings, disturbing,	45	–	45	7	38	–	5	4	35	45	–
Public park regulations, violation of,	164	5	169	9	20	140	47	70	21	169	–

Profane and obscene language, using,	—	161	43	35	50	28	104	29	161	12	149
Railroad law, violation of,	—	209	57	72	103	30	171	8	209	3	206
Runaways,	485	24	504	265	53	—	503	6	509	95	414
Refusing to pay car fare, etc.,	—	12	2	4	5	3	6	3	12	—	12
Registered label law, violation of,	—	1	—	—	1	1	—	—	1	1	—
Regulations of school committee, violation of,	—	4	1	—	2	1	—	3	4	1	3
Safe-keeping,	7	—	5	—	—	—	7	—	7	—	7
School law, violation of,	—	16	—	—	12	10	—	6	16	2	14
Signature, obtaining by fraud,	—	2	—	1	—	—	—	2	2	—	2
Shotgun or rifle, unlawful possession of,	—	3	—	—	3	—	3	—	3	—	3
Stragglers from United States navy or army.	251	—	81	231	15	—	251	—	251	—	251
Street car, disorderly conduct in,	—	13	3	11	7	—	9	4	13	—	13
Street railway transfers, misuse of,	—	11	1	—	9	5	—	6	11	1	10
Street traffic regulations, violation of,	—	1,789	167	865	528	1,694	50	45	1,789	9	1,780
Stubborn children,	—	139	139	3	11	24	3	112	139	57	82
Sunday law, violation of,	—	111	5	15	100	105	4	2	111	12	99
Suspicious persons,	1,667	—	540	516	490	—	1,667	—	1,667	34	1,633
Tobacco law, violation of,	—	5	—	1	2	3	—	2	5	1	4

TABLE XI — *Concluded.*

No. 8. OFFENCES NOT INCLUDED IN THE FOREGOING — *Concluded.*

NATURE OF OFFENCE.	Sex.		Total.	On Warrants.	Without Warrants.	Summoned by the Court.	Foreigners.	Non-residents.	Minors.	Held for Trial.	Discharged or to United States Authorities.
	Males.	Females.									
True name law, violation of,	119	97	216	171	42	3	74	73	17	216	-
United States army and navy uniform, wearing unlawfully.	4	-	4	-	4	-	-	3	2	-	4
United States flag law, violation of,	6	-	6	3	-	3	4	2	1	6	-
United States law, violation of (profiteering).	1	-	1	-	1	1	-	1	1	-	1
United States Navy regulations, violation of.	1	-	1	1	-	-	-	1	1	-	1
United States national defense act, violation of.	1	-	1	-	1	-	-	1	1	-	1
United States registration act, violation of.	2	-	2	-	2	-	2	1	1	-	2
United States selective service act, violation of (delinquent).	122	-	122	2	119	1	70	39	2	-	122
United States selective service act, violation of (section 13).	-	1	1	1	-	-	1	1	-	-	1
Vagrants, tramps, etc.,	150	5	155	25	129	1	56	104	15	155	-
Vagabond,	69	2	71	21	50	-	23	20	-	71	-
Vehicle light law, violation of,	132	-	132	3	-	129	55	26	38	132	-
Wage law, violation of,	2	-	2	1	-	1	2	-	-	2	-
Weights and measures, using falsely,	7	-	7	1	-	6	2	-	-	7	-

Winning more than $5 at card game, . . .	5	—	5	5	—	4	—	—	—	5	—
Wire law, violation of, . .	1	—	1	1	—	—	1	—	—	1	—
Witness, . . .	2	1	3	2	—	1	1	—	—	3	—
Totals, . .	52,989	3,632	56,621	2,866	43,734	10,021	20,391	24,778	7,613	53,389	3,232

RECAPITULATION.

No. 1, Offences against the person,	3,279	272	3,551	1,956	994	601	1,686	592	410	3,551	—
No. 2, Offences against property, committed with violence.	696	20	716	276	430	10	129	125	315	716	—
No. 3, Offences against property, committed without violence.	3,440	870	4,310	1,584	2,447	279	1,431	1,289	1,043	4,310	—
No. 4, Malicious offences against property.	133	13	146	76	33	37	45	22	45	146	—
No. 5, Forgery and offences against the currency.	82	7	89	64	—	25	19	37	20	89	—
No. 6, Offences against the license laws,	658	93	751	179	301	271	518	63	63	751	—
No. 7, Offences against chastity, etc., .	1,007	756	1,763	401	1,319	43	557	419	151	1,763	—
No. 8, Offences not included in the foregoing.	52,989	3,632	56,621	2,866	43,734	10,021	20,391	24,778	7,613	53,389	3,232[1]
Totals, . .	62,284	5,663	67,947	7,402	49,253	11,292	24,776	27,325	9,660	64,715	3,232[1]

[1] 637 to United States authorities.

TABLE XII.

Age and Sex of Persons arrested.

[Note. — "M", male, includes boys; "F," female, includes girls.]

OFFENCE.	Under 10		10 and under 15		15 and under 20		20 and under 25		25 and under 30		30 and under 35		35 and under 40		40 and under 45		45 and under 50		50 and under 55		55 and under 60		Over 60	
	M.	F.	M.	F.	M.	F.	M.	F.	M.	F.	M.	F.	M.	F.	M.	F.	M.	F.	M.	F.	M.	F.	M.	F.
No. 1,	–	–	12	–	304	14	732	56	659	51	520	46	418	32	239	31	189	19	97	12	60	8	49	3
No. 2,	–	–	11	–	269	6	218	3	77	4	41	1	31	3	20	1	16	–	7	2	1	–	5	–
No. 3,	–	–	41	–	684	128	763	222	563	160	418	99	337	85	241	61	182	57	104	29	51	17	56	12
No. 4,	–	–	1	–	41	–	41	1	10	3	6	2	12	3	6	2	4	1	7	1	5	–	–	–
No. 5,	–	–	–	–	11	2	19	3	15	–	18	1	11	1	4	–	–	–	3	–	1	–	–	–
No. 6,	–	–	4	–	36	1	77	6	79	16	132	7	99	19	75	16	71	12	38	9	28	5	19	2
No. 7,	–	–	–	–	44	49	220	218	180	164	176	120	134	106	99	48	83	34	36	13	18	3	17	1
No. 8,	246	63	1,966	137	4,291	354	6,688	351	7,029	404	6,909	439	7,240	575	5,545	447	5,697	388	3,502	237	2,035	123	1,841	114
Totals,	246	63	2,035	137	5,680	554	8,758	860	8,612	802	8,220	715	8,282	824	6,229	606	6,242	511	3,794	303	2,199	156	1,987	132

TABLE XIII.

Comparative Statement of Police Criminal Work 1915 to 1919, inclusive.

Years.	Estimated Population.	Number of Persons arrested.	Percentage of Arrests.	Amount of Property stolen in the City.	Amount of Property recovered stolen in and out of the City.	Amount of Fines imposed by Court.	Years of Imprisonment imposed by Court.	Number of Days' Attendance at Court.	Amount of Witness Fees earned.
1915,	770,599	88,762	11.51	$228,636 07	$291,289 43	$113,459 00	$3,753\frac{10}{12}$	45,447	$13,357 12
1916,	788,407	96,476	12.23	202,014 06	311,530 58	114,788 00	$3,328\frac{1}{12}$	48,222	12,401 45
1917,	802,853	108,556	13.52	388,329 16	462,240 98	124,252 50	$3,449\frac{6}{12}$	45,800	13,346 64
1918,	815,320	90,293	11.07	445,867 51	578,890 63	106,998 00	$2,615\frac{8}{12}$	40,124	11,260 15
1919,	826,938	67,947	8.21	1,415,485 79	1,238,206 26	107,325 00	$2,214\frac{8}{12}$	30,274	8,493 35
Averages,	800,823	90,407	11.31	$536,066 52	$576,431 57	$113,364 50	$3,072\frac{8}{12}$	41,973	$11,771 74

TABLE XIV.

Showing the Number of Licenses of all Kinds issued by the Police Commissioner and the Amount of Money received from all Sources and paid to the City Collector during the Year ending Nov. 30, 1919.

Class of License.	Applications received.	Licenses issued.	Rejected.	Transferred.	Canceled.	Revoked.	Complaints investigated.	Amount.
Auctioneer,[1]	175	171	4	3	—	—	9	$338 00
Chauffeur,	42	42	—	—	—	—	4	21 00
Dog,	8,292	8,292	—	—	—	—	59	21,457 00
Driver, hackney carriage,	1,867	1,858	9	—	56	9	195	929 00
Hackney carriage,	1,642	1,631	5	158	4	6	3	1,631 00
Hand cart,	62	58	—	—	—	—	—	58 00
Junk collector,	638	608	17	—	13	4	3	1,216 00
Junk-shop keeper,	161	148	13	10	15	1	4	740 00
Musician, collective,[2]	224	220	4	—	—	—	—	—
Musician, itinerant,	63	60	—	1	3	—	—	60 00
Pawnbroker,[3]	77	77	—	1	4	—	8	3,800 00
Private detective,	40	33	1	—	6	—	5	330 00
Public lodging house,[2]	10	10	—	—	—	—	—	—
Second-hand articles,	654	609	36	27	21	10	12	3,045 00
Sight-seeing automobiles,	24	24	—	3	—	—	—	395 00
Street railway conductors, motormen and starters,	1,014	1,014	—	—	1,736	—	2	253 50
Used cars,	150	142	2	25	6	—	2	1,775 00
Wagon,	5,204	5,131	3	—	92	—	2	5,131 00
Badges for itinerant musicians,							1	28 05
Badges for junk collectors,							—	94 35
Badges for special police,							—	135 00
Copies of licenses,							—	24 25
Received from Metropolitan Park Commission for food and cartage of prisoners,							—	128 00
Received from New England Telephone & Telegraph Company, commission on automatic pay station,							—	19 85
Rent of 38 Joy Street,							—	120 00
Sale of condemned property of the police department,							—	365 45
Sale of lost, stolen and abandoned property,							—	1,217 94
Sale of old listing cards and police lists,							—	16 62
Sale of pawnbrokers and second-hand articles report blanks,							—	405 50
Uniform cloth, etc.,							—	8,285 83
Contribution of citizens toward purchase of firearms,							—	7,977 20
Refund from Clarence A. Gleason,							—	21 00
Refund from Patrolman Thomas F. J. McGrade,							—	380 10
Totals,	20,339	20,128	94	227	1,956	30	306	$60,398 64

[1] Two veterans.   [2] No fee.   [3] Two at $25.

TABLE XV.

Number of Dog Licenses issued during the Year ending Nov. 30, 1919.

DIVISIONS.	Males.	Females.	Spayed.	Breeders.	Totals.
1, ...	23	2	–	–	25
2, ...	7	2	2	–	11
3, ...	147	59	15	2	223
4, ...	90	51	2	1	144
5, ...	277	114	16	2	409
6, ...	99	25	1	–	125
7, ...	392	75	13	–	480
9, ...	452	128	24	1	605
10, ...	343	87	22	–	452
11, ...	1,077	211	95	3	1,386
12, ...	338	80	27	–	445
13, ...	412	101	37	–	550
14, ...	487	127	66	2	682
15, ...	282	101	14	–	397
16, ...	492	130	48	–	670
17, ...	653	135	87	–	875
18, ...	313	58	18	–	389
19, ...	333	54	37	–	424
Totals, . .	6,217	1,540	524	11	8,292

TABLE XVI.

Total Number of Wagon Licenses issued in the City by Police Divisions.

Division 1, . . .	900	Division 12, . . .	75
Division 2, . . .	1,509	Division 13, . . .	74
Division 3, . . .	189	Division 14, . . .	70
Division 4, . . .	519	Division 15, . . .	169
Division 5, . . .	440	Division 16, . . .	113
Division 6, . . .	442	Division 17, . . .	54
Division 7, . . .	130	Division 18, . . .	79
Division 9, . . .	179	Division 19, . . .	15
Division 10, . . .	145		
Division 11, . . .	99	Total, ...	5,201

TABLE XVII.

Financial Statement for the Year ending Nov. 30, 1919.

EXPENDITURES.

Pay of police and employees, ...	$2,359,458 68
Pensions, ...	152,439 24
Fuel and light, ...	37,906 05
Water and ice, ...	1,001 16
Furniture and bedding, ...	4,123 23
Printing and stationery, ...	31,971 92
Care and cleaning station houses and city prison, .	9,342 71
Repairs to station houses and city prison, . .	8,764 13
Repairs and supplies for police steamers, . . .	30,736 97
Rent and care of telephones and lines, . . .	6,598 87
Purchase of horses and vehicles, ...	15,237 40
Care and keeping of horses, harnesses and vehicles, .	10,485 09
Care and repair of automobiles, ...	14,717 17
Transportation of prisoners, sick and insane persons,	1,146 10
Feeding prisoners, ...	2,800 57
Medical attendance on prisoners, ...	5,660 36
Transportation, ...	4,466 22
Pursuit of criminals, ...	6,217 81
Cloth for uniforms and uniform helmets, . .	36,296 27
Badges, buttons, clubs, belts, insignia, etc., . .	23,898 60
Traveling expenses and food for police, . .	10,100 24
Rent of buildings, ...	17,522 00
Legal services, ...	50 00
Total, ...	$2,790,940 79
Expenses of listing, ...	27,647 57
Expenses of house of detention and station house ma-trons, ...	14,087 52
Expenses of signal service (see Table XVIII), . .	72,111 59
Total, ...	$2,904,787 47

RECEIPTS.

For all licenses issued by the Police Commissioner, .	$19,722 50
For sale of unclaimed and condemned property, itin-erant musicians' badges, junk collectors' badges, carriage maps, etc., ...	2,956 11
For dog licenses (credited to school department), .	21,457 00
Total, ...	$44,135 61
For uniform cloth, etc., ...	8,285 83
Citizens' contribution to furnish arms for the depart-ment, ...	7,977 20
Total, ...	$60,398 64

TABLE XVIII.

Payments on Account of the Signal Service during the Year ending Nov. 30, 1919.

Labor, ...	$31,916 41
Hay, grain, shoeing, etc., ...	4,108 56
Rent and care of buildings, ...	5,071 04
Purchase of horses, harnesses and vehicles, ...	627 00
Stable supplies and furniture, ...	44
Repairs to buildings, ...	732 98
Repairing wagons, harnesses, etc., ...	17,625 49
Fuel, light and water, ...	1,454 34
Miscellaneous, car fares, etc., ...	660 71
Signaling apparatus, repairs and supplies therefor, . .	7,081 20
Underground wires, ...	2,791 63
Printing, stationery, etc., ...	41 79
Total, ...	$72,111 59

TABLE XIX.

Reports of Accidents in the Streets, Parks and Squares for the Year ending Nov. 30, 1919.

CAUSE.	DIVISION 1.		DIVISION 2.		DIVISION 3.		DIVISION 4.		DIVISION 5.		DIVISION 6.		DIVISION 7.		DIVISION 9.		DIVISION 10.		DIVISION 11.	
	Killed.	Injured.	Killed.	Injured.	Killed.	Injured.	Killed.	Injured.	Killed.	Injured.	Killed.	Injured.	Killed.	Injured.	Killed.	Injured.	Killed.	Injured.	Killed.	Injured.
Heavy carts,	-	14	-	58	-	-	-	1	-	-	-	7	-	3	1	3	-	5	1	1
Light carts,	-	22	-	7	-	7	-	1	-	3	-	11	-	10	1	7	-	2	1	4
Private carriages,	-	1	-	1	-	-	-	-	-	-	-	-	-	-	-	-	-	-	-	-
Licensed carriages,	-	-	-	3	-	-	-	-	-	-	-	-	-	-	-	-	-	-	-	-
Fire engines,	-	3	-	4	-	-	-	-	-	-	-	1	-	-	-	-	-	1	-	-
Bicycles,	-	-	-	3	-	4	-	-	-	4	-	6	1	5	-	2	-	1	-	4
Street cars,	-	4	-	27	-	4	-	16	-	19	-	14	5	37	-	23	1	3	2	18
Automobiles,	6	112	1	399	4	68	7	80	4	60	3	57	-	118	6	77	4	24	6	67
Defects in streets,	-	2	-	10	-	2	-	-	-	-	-	6	-	5	-	2	-	-	-	-
Falling objects,	-	17	-	22	-	8	-	12	-	1	-	3	-	1	-	4	-	69	-	7
Falls, various causes,	1	47	1	65	4	55	3	87	12	12	-	52	1	46	2	64	-	6	9	53
Excavations in streets,	-	1	-	1	-	-	-	10	-	-	-	4	-	-	1	2	-	25	-	-
Railroad trains,	-	-	-	-	-	-	-	-	-	-	-	-	-	-	-	5	-	4	-	-
Snow and ice on sidewalk,	-	-	-	-	-	-	-	-	-	-	-	-	-	-	-	2	-	-	-	-
Coasting,	-	-	-	-	-	-	-	-	-	-	-	-	-	13	-	2	-	1	-	-
Bitten by dog,	-	-	-	-	-	-	-	-	-	-	-	-	-	-	-	1	-	-	-	-
Jumped from window,	-	-	-	-	-	-	-	-	-	-	-	-	-	-	-	-	-	-	-	-
Kicked by horse,	-	-	-	-	-	-	-	-	-	-	-	-	-	-	-	6	-	-	-	-
Motor cycles,	-	-	-	2	-	-	-	-	-	-	-	-	-	2	-	1	-	2	-	-
Patrol wagon,	-	-	-	-	-	5	-	-	-	-	-	-	-	12	-	-	-	-	-	-
Runaway horse,	-	-	-	-	-	1	-	-	-	-	-	-	-	-	-	-	-	-	-	-
Shot or stabbed,	-	-	-	-	-	1	-	-	-	-	-	-	-	-	-	15	-	-	-	-
Coal hole,	-	-	-	-	-	-	-	-	-	-	-	-	-	-	-	-	-	-	-	-
Burns,	-	-	-	-	-	-	-	-	-	-	-	-	-	-	-	-	-	-	-	-
Aeroplane,	-	-	-	-	-	-	-	-	-	-	-	-	-	-	-	-	-	-	-	-
Total killed,	7	-	2	-	8	-	10	-	16	-	3	-	7	-	11	-	5	-	20	-
Total injured,	-	223	-	602	-	152	-	207	-	99	-	161	-	252	-	218	-	142	-	154

TABLE XIX — *Concluded.*

CAUSE.	Division 12. Killed.	Division 12. Injured.	Division 13. Killed.	Division 13. Injured.	Division 14. Killed.	Division 14. Injured.	Division 15. Killed.	Division 15. Injured.	Division 16. Killed.	Division 16. Injured.	Division 17. Killed.	Division 17. Injured.	Division 18. Killed.	Division 18. Injured.	Division 19. Killed.	Division 19. Injured.	Total killed.	Total injured.
Heavy carts,	—	1	—	1	—	1	—	2	—	1	—	1	1	—	—	—	3	96
Light carts,	—	3	—	1	—	1	—	8	—	2	—	1	—	—	—	3	1	93
Private carriages,	—	—	—	—	—	—	—	—	—	2	—	—	—	—	—	—	—	5
Licensed carriages,	—	—	—	—	—	—	—	—	—	—	—	—	—	—	—	—	—	4
Fire engines,	—	1	—	2	1	—	—	3	—	1	—	2	—	1	1	1	1	17
Bicycles,	1	10	4	3	—	15	4	1	1	23	1	11	—	4	3	9	15	31
Street cars,	3	43	—	42	1	79	—	8	7	215	4	53	3	22	4	64	92	269
Automobiles,	—	—	—	—	9	5	1	79	—	5	—	2	1	2	—	1	1	1,704
Defects in streets,	—	7	—	2	—	3	—	1	—	6	—	10	—	1	2	3	2	41
Falling objects,	—	10	—	19	1	25	—	42	—	—	—	1	—	1	1	1	23	104
Falls, various causes,	—	4	—	—	1	2	1	1	1	41	—	1	—	—	—	—	2	657
Excavations in streets,	—	—	—	—	—	—	—	—	—	—	—	—	—	—	—	—	—	30
Railroad trains,	—	1	—	—	—	1	—	—	7	—	—	—	—	—	—	1	—	13
Snow and ice on sidewalk,	—	—	—	—	—	—	—	—	—	—	—	—	—	—	—	—	—	6
Coasting,	—	—	—	—	—	—	—	—	—	—	—	—	—	—	—	—	—	4
Bitten by dog,	—	—	—	—	—	—	1	—	—	—	—	2	—	—	—	—	—	15
Jumped from window,	—	—	—	—	—	—	—	—	—	—	—	—	—	—	—	—	—	1
Kicked by horse,	—	2	—	—	—	—	—	—	—	—	—	—	—	—	—	2	—	10
Motorcycles,	—	—	—	3	—	4	—	—	—	—	—	—	—	—	—	3	—	27
Patrol wagon,	—	—	—	—	—	—	—	—	—	—	—	—	—	—	—	—	—	2
Runaway horse,	—	—	—	—	—	—	—	—	—	—	—	—	—	—	—	—	—	8
Shot or stabbed,	—	—	—	—	—	—	—	—	—	—	—	—	—	—	—	—	—	16
Coal hole,	—	—	—	—	—	—	—	—	—	—	—	—	—	—	—	—	—	1
Burns,	—	—	—	—	—	—	1	—	—	—	—	—	—	—	—	—	—	—
Aeroplane,	—	—	—	—	—	—	1	—	—	—	—	—	—	—	2	2	2	2
Total killed,	4		4		12		6		8		5		5		11		144	
Total injured,		82		73		135		145		295		95		32		89		3,156

TABLE XX.

Showing the Number of Male Persons, Twenty Years of Age or More, who were Residents of the City of Boston on the First Day of April, 1919, listed by the Listing Board in the Several Wards and Precincts of said City during the First Seven Week Days in April, 1919.

WARD.	Precinct 1.	Precinct 2.	Precinct 3.	Precinct 4.	Precinct 5.	Precinct 6.	Precinct 7.	Precinct 8.	Precinct 9.	Precinct 10.	Precinct 11.	Totals.
Ward 1,	1,121	963	688	771	894	760	982	1,025	—	—	—	7,213
Ward 2,	984	1,149	928	1,587	1,288	2,211	1,154	904	—	—	—	10,205
Ward 3,	1,015	854	824	823	776	614	686	—	—	—	—	5,457
Ward 4,	873	719	759	752	577	617	677	—	—	—	—	5,109
Ward 5,	4,983	4,383	3,178	2,948	1,817	1,357	3,098	—	—	—	—	21,764
Ward 6,	1,623	1,942	1,420	1,487	1,569	738	961	1,290	1,459	—	—	12,489
Ward 7,	927	1,744	1,846	1,459	1,800	1,665	1,323	1,561	1,358	—	—	13,683
Ward 8,	1,312	1,406	1,592	901	1,823	644	720	1,156	922	—	—	10,865
Ward 9,	1,134	949	795	1,004	1,093	1,038	865	840	803	—	—	8,640
Ward 10,	791	757	879	802	932	943	870	876	821	—	—	7,653
Ward 11,	941	857	817	673	804	1,268	830	906	904	—	—	7,917
Ward 12,	1,259	869	861	747	841	815	852	965	589	—	—	8,113
Ward 13,	1,318	1,126	1,126	1,085	898	785	844	800	713	—	—	8,571
Ward 14,	1,446	770	683	758	811	781	824	634	796	—	—	7,430
Ward 15,	886	914	995	917	839	854	867	725	924	—	—	7,793
Ward 16,	969	794	798	957	1,092	977	904	1,057	958	—	—	8,472
Ward 17,	817	744	1,035	796	985	740	1,204	771	768	—	—	8,050
Ward 18,	861	1,554	854	801	733	917	901	926	697	—	—	8,315
Ward 19,	946	928	1,118	805	1,028	773	828	686	741	—	—	7,809
Ward 20,	974	893	987	890	1,000	775	866	947	714	—	—	8,073
Ward 21,	1,637	1,388	1,212	918	901	729	774	750	1,028	—	—	9,023
Ward 22,	834	773	925	917	801	882	704	711	879	—	—	7,575
Ward 23,	915	816	800	813	762	764	879	781	—	—	—	7,409
Ward 24,	767	859	985	678	1,037	901	1,011	844	—	—	—	7,082
Ward 25,	974	810	1,456	2,042	1,089	837	—	—	—	—	—	7,208
Ward 26,	1,042	822	1,048	822	917	897	—	—	—	—	—	5,548
Total,												227,466

Table XXI.

Showing the Number of Women listed by the Listing Board in the Several Wards and Precincts of the City of Boston during the First Seven Week Days in April, 1919.

Ward.	Precinct 1.	Precinct 2.	Precinct 3.	Precinct 4.	Precinct 5.	Precinct 6.	Precinct 7.	Precinct 8.	Precinct 9.	Precinct 10.	Precinct 11.	Totals.
Ward 1,	53	38	59	13	36	32	79	99	–	–	–	409
Ward 2,	38	19	35	17	16	20	57	80	–	–	–	282
Ward 3,	59	96	79	41	54	118	89	–	–	–	–	536
Ward 4,	46	58	90	68	40	46	52	–	–	–	–	400
Ward 5,	8	11	3	49	40	22	43	17	27	–	–	176
Ward 6,	13	5	7	15	12	36	80	88	121	–	–	212
Ward 7,	73	36	31	63	45	27	55	99	71	–	–	539
Ward 8,	27	31	75	210	79	250	220	57	92	–	–	1,062
Ward 9,	44	32	54	57	30	52	63	42	96	–	–	481
Ward 10,	85	111	67	110	117	99	117	162	67	–	–	844
Ward 11,	39	36	21	59	98	61	107	71	151	–	–	650
Ward 12,	11	18	44	60	125	81	109	61	44	–	–	670
Ward 13,	20	14	29	21	75	32	27	43	86	–	–	323
Ward 14,	238	90	132	169	153	139	90	42	57	–	–	1,140
Ward 15,	63	82	119	30	27	56	44	69	118	–	–	520
Ward 16,	79	91	91	62	73	59	122	129	117	–	–	764
Ward 17,	55	61	32	92	142	91	82	73	93	–	–	801
Ward 18,	43	31	92	127	138	120	60	163	134	–	–	777
Ward 19,	77	129	54	165	79	143	78	117	102	–	–	1,022
Ward 20,	55	54	122	121	148	94	81	101	46	–	–	894
Ward 21,	34	52	44	60	102	164	.88	74	115	–	–	691
Ward 22,	85	81	48	43	149	113	123	188	81	–	–	831
Ward 23,	92	109	51	101	127	159	193	86	–	–	–	1,101
Ward 24,	47	37	84	125	121	117	41	–	–	–	–	658
Ward 25,	74	91	70	120	156	120	–	–	–	–	–	631
Ward 26,	120	70	78	216	214	177	–	–	–	–	–	875
Total,	·	·	·	·	·	·	·	·	·	·	·	17,289

INDEX

INDEX.

A.

B.

150055

C.

F.

G.

H.

I.

O.

P.

W.

REPORT OF THE CITIZEN'S COMMITTEE APPOINTED BY MAYOR PETERS TO CONSIDER THE POLICE SITUATION

S - B   October 3, 1919.

Hon. Andrew J. Peters,

    Mayor of Boston,

        Boston, Massachusetts.

Dear Sir:

        Your Committee believes that Your Honor is
unlikely to have occasion to call upon it for further
assistance and, therefore, I am directed to transmit
herewith the Committee's report with the request that
it be considered the final report of the Citizen's
Committee.

        The Committee would have sent to you its re-
port before this, except that the report necessarily
deals chiefly with events before the strike and it seemed
to your Committee inopportune to report while the
State was engaged with the immediate task of assert-
ing its sovereignty defeating the strike and reestab-
lishing law and order.

        The Committee has stated the facts to Your
Honor in its report. It wishes further to express its
position upon the present situation, which is embodied
in the following resolution passed at its meeting held
this afternoon:-

RESOLVED: That the policemen of Boston were unjustified in leaving their posts; that it is vital for the preservation of law that officers of the law should not be permitted, by organization or otherwise, to become affiliated with any outside bodies, the rules or interest of which might conflict with such duty; and that the Committee fully supports the acts of the authorities in preserving law and order and towards defeating finally and conclusively the effort to enforce by strike the right of policemen to join the American Federation of Labor.

Yours very truly,

(Signed) James J. Storrow,

Chairman, Citizen's Committee

Enclosure.

REPORT OF CITIZENS' COMMITTEE

TO

HON. ANDREW J. PETERS, MAYOR OF BOSTON

October 3, 1919.

Your Honor:

On August twenty-seventh you appointed a committee
of thirty-four citizens (Appendix 1) to co-operate with you
in dealing with the situation created by the action of the
patrolmen of the Boston police force in affiliating with
the American Federation of Labor.

It seems proper that the Citizens' Committee should
now submit to you a report of its labors, setting forth in
chronological order such published statements, official documents and acts of the committee, and the public officials
concerned, as may be necessary to give clearly the sequence
of the more material facts or events leading up to the strike.

On August twenty-seventh you issued a statement, published in all the papers, setting forth your attitude as Mayor
of the city. We quote from that statement:

> "The issue between the Commissioner and
> the policemen is clear-cut. It is the ques-
> tion of whether the policemen have a right to
> form a union and become affiliated with the
> A. F. of L."

****

> "The A.F. of L. deserves our coöperation
> and support in every proper way, but I do not
> think the policemen of any of our states or
> municipalities should become affiliated with it.
> This, as I understand it, is Commissioner Curtis'
> attitude, and in this I think he is right."
> (Appendix 2).

On the same day you appointed the Citizens' Committee.

On August twenty-eighth, James J. Storrow, who had
been requested by you to accept the chairmanship of the
committee, before accepting the position communicated un-
officially with the Police Commissioner to ascertain whether
he favored the appointment of the Citizens' Committee, and
whether it would be agteeable to him that Mr. Storrow should
serve as chairman or if he would prefer some other citizen.
The Commissioner's reply was tht he would be glad to see
the committee appointed, and glad to have Mr. Storrow serve
as chairman.

On August twenty-eighth the chairman of the Citizens'
Committee issued a statement to the effect that the policemen
should not affiliate with the A.F. of L. (Appendix 3).
Before this statement was issued it was informally submitted
to the Police Commissioner for suggestion or criticism, and
was approved by the Commissioner, who suggested only a slight
verbal change involving a word or two, which the chairman accept-
and made before the statement was issued.

On August twenty-ninth the Citizens' Committee met and
unanimously approved the statement issued by the chairman on
the preceding day, and also unanimously went on record as
against the affiliation of the Boston policemen with the A.
F. of L. (Appendix 4). The Committee also completed its
organization by the creation of the following Executive Committee:

George E. Brock
John R. Macomber
P.A. O'Connell
James J. Phelan
A. C. Ratshesky
Frederic S. Snyder
B. Preston Clark, Secretary
James J. Storrow, Chairman

On August twenty-ninth a letter was received by the chairman from James H. Vahey, counsel for the policemen's union, and the chairman's reply brought about a conference (Appendix 5).

A conference between George E. Brock, James J. Phelan and James J. Storrow, representing the Citizens' Committee, and the officers and counsel of the policemen's union began on the morning of August thirtieth and lasted during the three days of August thirtieth, August thirty-first and September first.

At these conferences the position of the committee was one of scrupulous, rigid and unyielding adherence to the Commissioner's and Mayor's position that the men must give up their A. F. of L. Charter; that on no basis could their retention as policemen be countenanced; that if the men should strike the committee would do the utmost in their power to see that they were defeated.

The men and their counsel stressed the long hours, the inadequate pay, the six years of service before the full rate of pay was attained, and the discomfort and unfitness of many of the older station houses. They also urged the inadequacy, proved through a long series of years, of their previous local organization known as the Boston Policemen's Social Club to effect any betterment in these conditions.

It should also be stated that at no time at any conference either with the police officials or their counsel did the committee, or the chairman, or any member of the comittee ever discuss the question of what increase in pay the men would like, or should or might be given, nor what reduction in hours should be made, if any.

On Labor Day, September first, the sub-committee which was holding these discussions with the police union officials and their counsel asked for a conference with the commissioner. The Committee were received with tye utmost courtesy by the Commissioner, who came to town from his summer residence to meet them. The only suggestion made by the Commissioner which seemed to bear in any way on the discussions which the Committee was holding with the police union officials and their counsel was the statement made by the Commissioner that the captains, lieutenants and other officers of the police force should receive exactly the same per cent. of increase in their pay as might be granted to the patrolmen. This struck the committee as proper and fitting, and at no time did the committee take or contemplate taking any action or position at wariance with the Commissioner's request in this regard.

By September second (Tuesday) although no definite adjustment had been worked out, the Executive Committee (with the exception of Mr. Macomber who was absent) had arrived at the opinion that an adjustment could be worked out with the officials and their counsel which would thoroughly uphold the Commissioner and the Mayor in their position that the

policemen must sever their connection with the A. F. of L.,
and at the same time bring about an amicable settlement of
the whole matter without a strike.

Though the Commissioner had as yet made no accounce-
ment, it was then understood by the committee that he was
expecting to announce his decision on Thursday morning, September fourth, in regard to the men on trial for affiliating
with the A. F. of L.

It was clear to the committee that finding the nineteen men guilty Thursday morning and proceeding to impose
punishment at roll call that afternoon would end these discussions, put a stop to further consideration on the part of
the policemen of a voluntary withdrawal from the A. F. of L.,
and at once precipitate a strike.

Accordingly a letter signed by the chairman of the
Citizens' Committee, requesting a brief postponement of the
decision, was presented to the Commissioner Wednesday morning
at the Commissioner's office by a member of the committee.
No action was taken in response nor reply received to this
letter, because counsel for the Commissioner who received
and read the letter declined to permit its delivery to the
Commissioner. (See copy of letter, Appendix 6).

At the close of the conference following presentation
of the letter, the Commissioner sent word to counsel
for the police officials that he would read his decision
the following morning at nine forty-five. That same evening,
feeling that an avoidable strike was impending, and

because under our laws the control and government of the
Boston police force is vested in the state and not in the
hands of the municipal authorities, a conference was sought
with the Governor and attended on behalf of the Citizens'
Committee by Charles G. Bancroft, Charles G. Bancroft, Charles
F. Choate, B. Preston Clark, James J. Phelan, George E. Brock and
the chairman. The Governor, however, stated to the representatives of the committee that he felt it was not his duty to
communicate with the Commissioner on the subject.

The next morning, and before the announced hour of
the Commissioner's decision, the Mayor made a formal request for
a delay in the proceedings (Appendix 7). This letter was
presented to counsel for the Commissioner by Your Honor, who
was accompanied by Mr. Charles F. Choate, counsel of and
member of the Citizens' Committee. The Commissioner thereafter announced that his decision was adjourned from that
Thursday morning until Monday, September eighth, at nine-
fifteen o'clock.

On Thursday afternoon, September fourth, Mr. Choate
drew and presented to Messrs. Vahey and Feeney a preliminary
draft of what was intended to provide an amicable adjustment
of the controversy on the basis of a voluntary surrender of
the A. F. of L. charter.

On September sixth this preliminary draft was revised
into a final plan (Appendix 8) embodied in the letter of the
sixth of September to Your Honor and signed that afternoon by
all the members of the Executive Committee except Mr. John R.
Macomber, who was out of the state and inaccessible, but who

upon his return approved the plan.

This plan had as its first clause and starting point the turning back by the Boston Police Union to the American Federation of Labor of the charter which had been obtained from that organization by the Boston Police Union. As the committee never discussed with either the police officials or their counsel what the wages of the men should be, or what the hours of the men should be, this plan did not undertake to fix either of these things. It did not even provide for decisive arbitration of these matters. The second clause did provide a Committee of Information consisting of three citizens to be appointed by the concurrent action of the Commissioner, the Mayor and the local police organization which would exist after the surrender of the charter. This second clause provided simply that one copy of the report of this Committee of Information should be filed with the Commissioner, one copy with the Mayor and that one copy should be published for the information of the citizens of Boston. The report neither had nor purported to have any binding effect upon the city, the Mayor, or upon the Commissioner. The two clauses referred to above give the keynote to the report, and it does not seem necessary to go into further detail, as the full report is given in the Appendix (Appendix 8). It was specifically provided in the report that the provisions of Section 2 calling for a committee of three citizens "shall not apply to any questions of discipline". The plan embodied in this letter was submitted to the Mayor Saturday afternoon, September sixth, and was approved by him. The plan was also informally offered that afternoon to the Commissioner for his consideration, criticism and suggestion. No action was taken by the Commissioner. Your Honor thereupon decided formally to submit the plan as approved by Your Honor to the Commissioner for consideration and this was done by letter dated September sixth (Appendix 9). This letter was delivered to the Commissioner at his residence at nine o'clock the next morning, Sunday, September seventh.

As Your Honor heard nothing from the Commissioner in reply during Sunday and as the time limit set by the Commissioner for delivering his finding in regard to the nineteen officers on trial would expire at nine-fifteen on Monday morning, and as Your Honor knew this would precipitate a strike, you decided on Sunday evening after conference with your Committee that the plan should be given to the citizens of Boston in Monday's papers and this was accordingly done. The plan was heartily approved by the morning papers of the city and by all the afternoon papers except one, as thoroughly upholding the basis principle of the surrender of the American Federation of Labor charter, and yet providing a method affording the patrolmen a reasonable prospect that their grievances would receive consideration.

It is true that in the brief space of time between Saturday afternoon when this plan finally took shape and nine-fifteen Monday morning there had hardly been time for the members of the police union to reach a final determination as to whether they would surrender their charter and accede to the

plan, yet the Executive Committee (Mr. Macomber still being out
of the city)was clearly of the opinion that on Sunday the plan
was on the point of being approved by their officials, and that
it would also be approved at a general meeting of the men. The
opinion of your committee in this regard was also confirmed by
the fact that the counsel for the Police Union, Messrs. Vahey
and Feeney, both unqualifiedly advised the officials to accept
it, and also undertook to attend the general meeting of all
the members of the Police Union and there unqualifiedly to
advise the men to accept it. Such a meeting could and would
have been held probably on Monday afternoon, September eighth,
but instead of considering your committee's plan on Monday afternoon, the men as the result of the Commissioner's finding
of that morning (following his earlier declination to consider
the plan) thereupon entered upon the business of taking a
strike vote. This committee does not seek in this report to
express opinion as to whether the Commissioner was or was not
justified in declining to adopt this plan, but merely to record
the history of their endeavors to present what seemed to them
to be a sound and constructive solution of the situation.

The Commissioner's formal answer to Your Honor's letter
recommending the plan for consideration is given in the Appendix
(Appendix 10). This committee wishes to state that in every conference the utmost courtesy was exhibited by representatives of
the police organization in presenting their views and considering
the views of the representatives of the committee. Messrs. Vahey
and Feeney, counsel for the Police Union, were not counsel at the
time the men became affiliated with the American Federation of

Labor, but were retained and brought into consultation subsequently when the nineteen police officers were placed on trial. In view of various allegations which appeared in some of the papers it also seems proper to say that all the members of the committee who came into contact with Messrs. Vahey and Feeney as counsel for the men are of opinion that counsel for the men exerted every honorable means in their power to coöperate with your committee in order to find a way out of the apparent impasse in which the men had become involved when before receiving the advice of counsel they joined the American Federation of Labor.

An endeavor had been made by your committee on Sunday, September seventh, to obtain a second conference with the Governor for the purpose of reporting upon the then critical situation and presenting for his consideration the committee's plan. But the Governor was reported to be in the western part of the state and such a conference could not be arranged. On Monday, September eighth, the Mayor in coöperation with the members of your committee again endeavored to obtain a conference with the Governor, and such a conference was arranged to take place early in the evening of that day. At that time the Commissioner had taken final action in regard to the police officials. Your committee in collaboration with Your Honor thereupon advised the Governor of the entire situation, presenting the plan and stating its status. Constructive action upon the principles proposed was urged. In the absence of such action Your Honor and the members of your committee emphasized the prospective seriousness of the

situation which would result from the absence of the great majority of the patrolmen and expressed their strong conviction as to
the necessity of troops to the number of not less than three to
four thousand to be present in Boston on the day following at
5:45 P.M. either upon the streets or ready in the armories.

The members of the committee at this conference were:

> Gen. Charles H. Cole
> B. Preston Clark
> George E. Brock
> John R. Macomber
> Frederic S. Snyder
> P. A. O'Connell
> A. C. Ratshesky
> James J. Storrow

On Tuesday, September ninth, at about one o'clock, Your
Honor, as set forth in your letter to the chairman
(Appendix 15) visited the Commissioner at his office in
Pemberton Square, and was assured by the Commissioner that
he had the situation well in hand and had ample means at his
disposal for the protection of the city. Your Honor asked
him whether he did not think he ought to have the State Guard
ready for emergencies, and the Commissioner replied that he
did not need it and did not want it. (Appendix 16 and 17).
Your Honor then suggested to the Commissioner that the Governor's
consideration of the question of protection of the city should
be asked. The Commissioner replied that it was not necessary,
but consented to see the Governor with the Mayor. At this
conference the same ground was gone over again. The Police
Commissioner reiterated his assurances that he had the situation
in hand and had made ample provision, and again stated that he
did not need or want the State Guard. No action was taken.

The volunteer police were not called to duty until Wednesday morning. On Tuesday evening, September ninth, riots, disorders and robbery occurred, and on Wednesday morning, September tenth, Your Honor assumed temporary control of the Police Department, acting under the Statute of 1917, Ch. 327, Part 1, Sec. 26 (Appendix 19), which gives Your Honor the power to do so, "tumult" having then occurred. Your Honor also immediately called out that part of the State Guard located in Boston which you then had authority to do, and requested the Governor to order out three additional regiments of infantry.

On Wednesday morning, September tenth, it was clear to the members of your committee that the situation had become a military one, and that there was nothing further your committee could do except to assist in securing trucks and other conveyances for the State Guard, which duty your committee immediately undertook. The prompt and patriotic response of business concerns to our request for trucks to move troops and supplies should be highly commended.

Your committee also, at the request of the Mayor, undertook the task of aiding the Fire Commissioner to prepare for the possible contingency of a strike of firemen.

All discussions of a peaceful solution of the difficulty necessarily ended with the conference held with the Governor Monday night, September eighth. No negotiations or attempted negotiations with the police officials or their counsel in regard to an amicable settlement were held after that time.

It was also true, of course, that by Wednesday morning, September tenth, your committee could contribute nothing in the way of publicity to bring our citizens to see that it was undesirable for the policemen to affiliate with the American Federation of Labor because by Wednesday morning the preponderance of opinion against the policemen joining the American Federation of Labor, or exercising the right to strike, was overwhelming.

By Thursday morning order had been generally restored in the city. On Thursday afternoon, September eleventh, the Governor assumed control of the situation, as indicated by his proclamation of that day (Appendix 27).

In fairness to all parties, it should be stated that, although a majority of the Executive Committee of your Committee formed opinions as above set forth, yet at no time did the Executive Committee of the union, or the members of the union vote to surrender their union affiliation or in any other way act upon the matter, except by vote to strike following the suspension of the nineteen members who were placed upon trial.

And in justice to the Commissioner it should further be stated that at no time during the progress of the affair did counsel for the union or officers of the union or men upon trial take any position with the Commissioner other than to insist upon continuing and retaining their membership in the union.

And in justice to the Governor it should be stated

That at all times he assured the members of your committee
that whenever called upon for a military force he would provide sufficient men – if they could be secured – to maintain
law and order.

And in further justice to all parties it should be
stated that the Governor, the Mayor, and the Commissioner,
in the opinion of the committee, acted at all times from the
highest of motives and with but a single thought; namely,
the welfare of the Commonwealth and its people.

Respectfully submitted,

EXECUTIVE COMMITTEE

(Signed) George E. Brock

" John R. Macomber

" P. A. O'Connell

" James J. Phelan

" A. C. Ratshesky

" Frederic S. Snyder

" B. Preston Clark, Secretary

" James J. Storrow, Chairman

The Chairman has been asked by Messrs. Brock, O'Connell
and Snyder, who are out of the state today, but who have each
of them read the report, to affix their names to the report.

(Initialed) J.J.S.

Governor Coolidge's monopoly of law and order.

One would think in reading Republican speeches and paid advertisements in the newspapers that anybody who voted against Governor Coolidge was an anarchist, and that only those who voted for him believed in law and order. It is claimed for him that because of his conduct in the Boston Police strike he deserves the commendation of all law abiding citizens, and that those who disagree with him should be condemned.

It has been said that in the western part of Massachusetts where he lives everyone of all political parties, except those who believe in lawlessness, violence and a reign of terror, would vote for him for Governor.

I have ventured to come out here and tell the people of western Massachusetts the truth. I am very certain that the newspapers out here will be fair enough to print honest criticism of him that is supported by testimony of the greatest proof and the highest character. Is Governor Coolidge a hero? Is he an apostle of law and order? Is he a disciple of righteousness? Does he occupy such an eminence with respect to these civic virtues that it is unassailable?

You people who are his neighbors, and many of you his friends, will not hesitate to condemn him if he is wrong, no more than you have failed to praise him when he was right.

The truth has never been told to the people of western
Massachusetts concerning the Boston police strike. It
is time that it should be told.

The Boston policemen for 15 years were getting
low wages and worked long hours under burdensome conditions.
They had an organization called the "Social Club" which re-
dressed no grievance; brought about no relief; was controlled
by Headquarters and was absolutely useless as a means of im-
proving the economic conditions of the members of the police
force. Neither Commissioner O'Meara nor Commissioner Curtis ob-
jected to the formation of a union of the Boston policemen.
Both of them knew that the social club meant nothing in the way
of securing reform. The burdens of the policemen and their
families had become very heavy. They were getting from 21¢
to 30¢ an hour a day. They worked 19 and 20 hours for a
day's pay, with nothing for overtime. They were compelled
to sleep in unsanitary Station Houses, which were filled with
vermin. They were sometimes compelled to sleep in beds in
which three men in succession had slept without being made up.

They resented these conditions. They formed a union.
They affiliated with the American Federation of Labor, and not
until after the formation of their union and their affiliation
with the American Federation of Labor, did the present police
commissioner promulgate any rule prohibiting them.

The law of Massachusetts is; Section 19, Chapter 514,
Acts of 1909----- "No person shall himself or by his agent
coerce or compel a person into a written or oral agreement not to join or become a member of a labor organization as
a condition of his securing employment or continuing in the employment of such person".

That is now a law of Massachusetts. It has never been
changed. Our courts have not construed it. A similar
statute in the State of Kansas was declared to be unconstitutional by a vote of 5 justices to 4. Oliver Wendell Holmes,
for many years chief justice of the Supreme Court of Massachusetts, was one of the 4 men who voted for its constitu-
tionality. Since that time the Supreme Court bench of the
United States has been humanized. Many changes have been made.
Oliver Wendell Holmes is still there, as are also Justice Brandeis
and Justice Clark. It is extremely probable that such a statute
would be declared to be constitutional by the Supreme Court of
the United States as at present composed.

Commissioner Curtis violated this law, which carries
with it a criminal penalty. Section 36 of the same act says
"Whoever violates a provision of this act, for which no specific
penalty is provided, shall be punished by a fine of not more than
$100.00"

Governor Coolidge made no criticism of this violation of law and order. Long before any strike took place Mayor Peters appointed a committee of 34, two-thirds of whom were Republicans, and friends of the Governor. Mr. James J. Storrow, a member of the firm of Lee, Higginson & Company, was the chairman. He asked Commissioner Curtis if he was willing that he should serve. Commissioner Curtis said that he was. This Committee recommended a plan which I read to you.

This plan was approved by the whole Committee, Mayor Peters, the Boston Chamber of Commerce and every newspaper in Boston, except one. The Governor declined to do a single thing to aid the adoption of the plan. He declined to help. He declined to order out the State Guard. He left the City of Boston defenseless and unprotected, although the Mayor of Boston had been assured by the Governor and the Commissioner that there was ample provision made for the emergency of the policemen's strike. From Monday night until Thursday afternoon Governor Coolidge didn't lift a finger and did not attempt to stop the tumult and riot and disorder which was prevalent in Boston, until after it was over. He was a general who led his troops onto the battlefield after the battle had been fought, and everybody had gone home to bed.

Let him call the roll of the nine dead, and ask himself what his responsibility is for their death. Let him in his inner conscience ask himself what he did to prevent the Boston police strike. If the President of the United States was not doing from his sick bed everything he could to avert the Miners' strike; if he wasn't doing from his sick bed everything he could to prevent a food shortage, would he be criticised? The Governor of Massachusetts clothed with the power to remove the Police Commissioner if he failed in his great public duty could on the 9th day of September have removed Commissioner Curtis. The Council would have failed in its duty if it didn't approve his act, and he would have stopped a strike which was his duty to prevent so that Boston would not become a city of shame and disgrace.

The Boston Herald now so loyally proclaiming Governor Coolidge's praises said on the day following the strike that someone in authority had blundered.

<u>EDITORIALS OF BOSTON NEWSPAPERS COMMENTING ON</u>

<u>PLAN OF CITIZENS' COMMITTEE</u>

Boston Globe, September 8, 1919.

<u>Solving the Police Difficulty</u>

The proposition put forward by the Citizens' Committee appointed by the Mayor seems to offer a very workable solution of the police situation.

It does not take away from the disciplinary power of the Commissioner, and it does afford a method for the police to get a hearing at any time on any grievances they may have.

The Commissioner is on record as not opposing an organization among the policemen themselves, and the proposed plan provides for this.

For either the Commissioner or the police to refuse this solution of the difficulty would be a grave mistake.

The plan in its present form, or as it may be amended along similar lines, is worthy of a trial and should at least have its chance.

A strike under these conditions is unthinkable, and the sympathetic strikes which might follow would set back the principle of collective negotiation immeasurably.

The public at large will recognize the fairness of
the proposition of the Citizens' Committee, and the people are,
after all, the court of last resort, and their interests are
entitled to first consideration.

Boston Herald, September 8, 1919.

The Strike Compromise

The Mayor's committee, of which Mr. Storrow is the
chairman, has made a report on the police situation which
appears on the front page this morning. It is a compromise.
It gives the patrolmen everything they ask except affiliation
with the American Federation of Labor, and since they sought
that only as a device for bettering their condition, they have
presumably gained everything. The report provides for the
formation of a Boston policemen's union, which will give the
necessary outlet for negotiations as to wages and hours and
other conditions of life. It calls for an immediate survey of
the policemen's lot, with the strong implication that this
would be bettered.

We look to see the Commissioner and the patrolmen
accept this projected compromise. The latter, surely, can
ill afford to go out on a strike on the single issue of
affiliation with the American Federation, when they can have
everything else that they are in reason entitled to, without

that attachment. If they refuse to take this, instead of
insisting on a strike, they will have no public sentiment
behind them. Mr. Curtis, on his part, will be most generous
to accept this compromise, but we expect him to do so, and
should so advise him. Beyond that he ought not to go —
indeed can not go.

Boston Post, September 8, 1919

<u>A Wise Solution</u>

The report of the Mayor's Committee on the police
situation, indorsed by the Mayor, is a happy solution of the
whole difficulty. It provides a way for the police to organize which is thoroughly within the letter and the spirit of
the police commissioner's rules. It gives to the men of the
police force a broad and comprehensive approach toward a complete
settlement of all their grievances.

We believe that such a plan will commend itself to
the men of the force and to the commissioner as well, for
there is neither victory nor defeat in it.

It seems a common sense settlement for which the committee is entitled to credit. They have approached the subject in a broad-minded way, thoroughly in sympathy with many
of the claims of the men, and likewise, keenly alive to the
position of the commissioner.

The Post feels quite sure that this way out of the difficulty will be indorsed by the citizens of Boston as reasonable and wise. We trust it will be speedily agreed to by both sides.

Boston American, September 8, 1919

Compromise Suggested in Police Crisis Honorable and Just

The police situation is like the deadly calm that precedes the storm. No one should rock the boat. Least of all the public officials. No one should stand upon technical rights. It is a condition and not a theory that faces us.

The citizens' Committee has suggested a compromise which seems honorable and just, both to the official representatives of the public and to the men. The American believes that Commissioner Curtis was right in objecting to the police force assuming an obligation that might become inconsistent with their oath of office. On the other hand, the rights of the men have been neglected and postponed, and it is human nature that they should take the accepted method of enforcing their just demands. If there is a sincere interest on the part of the public officials to better the working conditions of the police force and to give them adequate wages under the plan suggested by the citizens' committee,

then upon the face of the plan it seems a happy way out of the
crisis.

Let no one get rattled, and neither shift position
in the boat violently nor keep up any sail that ought to be
reefed in view of the threatening skies.

Boston Evening Record, September 8, 1919

Public Safety Menaced as Curtis Ignores Peace Plan

A police strike is imminent and disorder is in consequence about to be turned loose upon this city because the
Police Commissioner elects to pursue his case to the extreme
of insistence rather than consider the welfare of the public.

The Commissioner has until 5 P.M. today to exert his
power to undo the evil which has been done. He has found certain members of the police force guilty of violation of a police rule made for the occasion. He has announced that he will
utter his judgment at 5 o'clock roll call. Upon the nature of
his utterance may depend the safety of the city.

The Police Commissioner appears to be under an unfortunate influence, with sinister consequences. Acting upon
whatever advice he regards as desirable, he has been unrecep-
tive to the efforts of the Mayor's special committee, apparently unable to recognize the fact that this committee is the
only voice of the public, and apparently unable to recognize
the fact that the public is the one party that must be served
in the matter.

The Police Commissioner is on record as agreeable to organization of the police among themselves, not affiliated with the A. F. of L. That the police have just grievances is true. Their hours are burdensome and their pay is inadequate. They have the right to some method of presenting those grievances. The Commissioner held that they had no right to affiliate with an outside organization; and this attitude of the Commissioner had public approval.

The Commissioner's present attitude, that a compromise recommendation which eliminates this outside affiliation and permits inside organization is not entitled to his favorable consideration, is hostile to the public interest, defiant of public opinion and menacing to public safety.

The case of the Boston policemen has at all times been susceptible to amicable adjustment, without a strike. The Mayor's special committee has worked to that end, and has presented a workable plan for solution. This plan the Commissioner, badly advised, has thrown in the waste basket.

The Record believes that the public resents being thrown in the waste basket by a Police Commissioner or by a legal adviser whose conception of the situation appears to be contaminated by an undue inflation of a plain matter of common sense and public welfare into a legal cause celebre.

1

LIST OF MEMBERS OF CITIZENS' COMMITTEE

James J. Storrow, Chairman
George W. P. Babb
Ezra H. Baker
Charles G. Bancroft
Edmund Billings
George E. Brock
Vincent Brogna
Dr. Arthur M. Broughton
Charles F. Choate
B. Preston Clark
Gen. Charles H. Cole
Howard Coonley
Henry V. Cunningham
T. J.Falvey
J.Wells Farley
Frank M. Eshleman
A. Lincoln Filene
Paul E. Fitzpatrick
Edward G. Graves
John T. Hosford
John R. Macomber
J. W. Maguire
Harry P. Nawn
#George R. Nutter
P. O. O'Connell
Joseph H. O'Neil
James J. Phelan
A. C. Ratshesky
Robert Seaver
Frederick S. Snyder
Charles F. Weed
Butler R. Wilson
Frank L. Young

#Mr. Nutter immediately after his appointment
was obliged to leave the state and was unable
to be present at the first or any subsequent
meeting.

2

MAYOR PETERS' STATEMENT WEDNESDAY, AUGUST 27

The issue between the commissioner and the policemen is clear cut. It is the question of whether the policemen have a right to form a union and become affiliated with the A. F. of L. The merits of this question are not perhaps so clear. All fair-minded people admit the right of any ordinary group of workers to organize and to become affiliated with some central or federated labor body, and, I am happy to say, most of us recognize not only that right, but the advantages to the workers, and in most instances, to the community from following such a course.

But it is argued that policemen are not, in this sense, ordinary workers; that they are in reality public officials, charged with the duty of impartially enforcing law and order, whose allegiance in their public capacity should be to their public duty alone. No one would deny them the privilege of forming among themselves an association which would enable them to secure the benefits of collective bargaining and such other advantages as organization brings. But when they take the further step of affiliating themselves with an outside body, which, however meritorious, represents only a portion of the public, it is easy to see that complications might, and probably would ensue, would not be in the public interest. Policemen are human, like the rest of us.

I am in entire sympathy with the fundamental aims of the A. F. of L. and believe it to be a wisely administered and progressively conservative organization. It is now a great, and I hope will steadily become, a greater bulwark of patriotism and strength to all not only from those who seek unrighteously to wield the power that money gives, but also from those who, through Bolshevism or some kindred fallacy, seek to overthrow our institutions.

The A. F. of L. Deserves our cooperation and support in every proper way, but I do not think that the policemen of any of our States or municipalities should become affiliated with it. This, as I understand it, is Commissioner Curtis' position, and in this I think he is right.

2 (Continued)

       I earnestly hope both the A. F. of L. and
the Boston police officers will voluntarily relinquish
their plan. If they do so, I feel that they will receive, in a greater degree than ever before, the commendation and support of the general public, and I am
certain that those of us who are in official positions
will at all times do all in our power to see that
justice is rendered to them.

3

STATEMENT OF
JAMES J. STORROW, CHAIRMAN CITIZENS' COMMITTEE
THURSDAY, AUGUST 28th

      I have accepted the Mayor's request to
serve as chairman of the Citizens' Committee somewhat
regretfully because I had planned this week to begin a
much needed rest but it seems to be my duty. At the
outset, I want to say I have not the faintest feeling
of antagonism to the police officers. Many officers
are my personal friends and during all my life I have
seen them courageously, honestly and honorably protect-
ing the life and limb and welfare of the citizens of
Boston. I am deeply grateful for what the police
officers have been quietly doing for me all these
years and I am only too glad to stand up and acknowl-
edge my debt.

      I have tried to get over on the side of the
fence on which our police officers stand and view this
question in a friendly, sympathetic manner from their
point of view. I now ask them to consider with open
mind and with care the views I have set forth. They
come from a well wisher and a friend.

      I do not see any objection to the police officers
of Boston forming their own independent and
unaffiliated organization so that they can put their
best men forward to bargain collectively with the city,

<u>3</u> (Continued)

and I understand not the slightest objection has been
raised to this. I am also certain that the citizens
of Boston hold them in high respect and will be interested in and assist them in remedying any inadequacy
of pay, overextended hours or tours of duty, or any
avoidable hardships or discomforts now incident to
their duty.

      The patriotism of the American Federation of
Labor during the war, under the lead of its president,
Samuel M. Gompers, cannot be questioned for one moment.
I have stated this repeatedly and I am glad to say it
again with all emphasis. As our Government advanced
to exert its utmost force in the mightiest war of all
ages, the American Federation of Labor stood absolutely
behind the Government and contributed every ounce of
strength it possessed to make that force the knock-out
blow for Germany. Indeed I need not go further than to
cite the work of the official labor representatives on
the Public Safety Committee of our own State. Again
and again we turned to them for advice and assistance.
In not one single instance in two long years of daily
intercourse did they fail to give us in the spirit of
the highest patriotism sound advice and splendid help,
and the labor organizations stood behind them to a man.

      The right of the workingmen of this country

<u>3</u> (Continued)

to create and maintain labor unions for their own
betterment and advancement cannot be questioned for
one moment. They have been one of the most potent
factors for the advancement of mankind ever conceived
and engineered by the mind and hand of man. It is
quite some years ago that, in my formal printed report
on the Elevated Railroad Arbitration, I stated that it
was altogether too late in the World's history to waste
a moment in discussing the right of the Elevated employees to organize a union.

Now we come to the question of whether our
police officers should join the American Federation of
Labor and become an integral part of it.

I have given this question the best, the most
impartial and the most sympathetic consideration I am
capable of exercising. I have also approached it with
entire respect for what appears to be the viewpoint of
a large number at least of the police officers of Boston.
I have lived long enough and seen enough of men to learn
by this time that a manly man is a man and that a little
extra veneer of education or of this or that cuts very
little ice in all these fundamental questions.

I cannot help remembering that when I was a young
law student I often walked into one of our criminal courts
and sat through a trial. The case sometimes would be one
of assault in the street. The most important witnesses

<u>3</u> (Continued)

would generally be the defendant and the officer.
What the other witnesses said did not as a rule amount
to much and in fact if it had been a case of rough work
in the street the officer would have been too busy cap-
turing his prisoner and getting him away from the scene
of the fracas to list up the other people present. Sometimes the alleged defendant and the officer would be the
only witnesses of any consequence and here the court
must plainly rely on the statement of the officer as the
only unbiased man and resolve the flat contradictions
in favor of the officer and sentence the defendant
accordingly.

In like manner if both parties to the assault
were present the case would be about the same. Each
man would say he was defending himself and that the other
attacked him and the word of the officer settled which one
of them went to jail and which one got off scot free.

Most of our citizens see our officers performing their duty in the street; they do not think of the
vital part of their duty performed in court as an unbiased and impartial officer of the law engaged in decid-
ing whether a man shall be sent to serve a sentence or
allowed to go home.

Many strikes have been carried through to a
finish without a vestige of violence. But on the other

<u>3</u> (Continued)

hand any fair-minded man knows that in many strikes
violence does crop out. It is the exception when
assaults and destruction of property are carried on
with either the encouragement or connivance of the
officers of the union. But under the excitement
and bias of a strike the hot heads often do what the
cooler heads and the responsible officers of the union
deplore. Sometimes it is the sympathizers and over-
zealous friends of the strikers who make the assaults,
break the windows andoccasionally go so far as to
threaten bodily injury to innocent parties having no
connection with the strike.

I do not question the good faith of the police
officers in believing that in a strike in which the American Federation of Labor is involved they can preserve an
absolutely judicial and unbiased attitude between those who
are their fellow members of the American Federation of
Labor and other members of the community who are not.
But, indeed, I have lived too long to feel I can safely
be subjected to special bias or sympathy for men on one
side of a controversy and then be sure it has no effect
on my views and actions. A man can not always tell when
he is being perfectly fair. We have all seen lots of
men who we knew intended to be absolutely fair in their
statements and positions and yet it has been as plain to

3 (Continued)

I think every man in Boston would agree that
it would not be proper for our judges to join a labor
union. For hundreds of years justice has been depicted
as holding the scales with eyes blindfolded. This has
not been an idle thought. It means that ever since
man became sufficiently civilized to establish courts
of law, the universal consensus of opinion demanded that
the machinery of our tribunals should operate without
partiality and as near as is humanly possible without a
tinge of bias for one man, or against another.

But any man who thinks that our judges should
not become affiliated with a labor organization must, so far
as I can see, reach the same conclusion in regard
to the police officer. The police officer is engaged in
the administration of the law as well as the judge. He
is a part of it. His influence in sending the right or
the wrong man to jail is oftentimes not less than that of
the judge. If partisanship consciously or unconsciously
warps the testimony of the officer, the judge cannot necessarily correct it. The judge is not a witness; he must
convict or free a man on the evidence as given, and the
account given by the police officer of what happened must
weigh heavily with the judge and again and again settle
the defendant's fate.

There are many other points I might mention
which have led me to my conclusion that our police officers

3 (Continued)

should not join the American Federation of Labor.
Suppose a police officer could be sure he has handled
a case without bias and we will assume that, although
his sympathy is on one side, still he has actually succeeded
in showing not the slightest partiality, yet in
a time of excitement and angry feelings how are the
rest of us to know he has been successful in suppressing
his feelings? Our courts of justice must nnt only
administer exact justice to all, but it is vital that
their findings when made should be beyond question or
suspicion. Justice is depicted not merely with her eyes
closed, but to put her impartiality beyond cavil her
eyes are blindfolded.

<u>4</u>

<u>RESOLUTIONS ADOPTED AT FIRST MEETING OF</u>
<u>CITIZENS' COMMITTEE, AUG. 29th</u>

<u>Resolved</u>: that the Citizens' Committee record its admiration of the Boston Police Force as a body of men which has won the respect and confidence of the whole community through years of firm, courteous, impartial and faithful service.

<u>Resolved</u>: that the Citizens' Committee express its recognition of the sane, effective and patriotic services rendered the country by the American Federation of Labor.

<u>Resolved</u>: that the Citizens' Committee is not opposed to any organization by the members of the Boston Police Force within its own body.

<u>Resolved</u>: that the Citizens' Committee is opposed to the affiliation by any organization of the Boston Police Force with the American Federation of Labor for the reason that such affiliation tends to divide the allegiance of a body of men which in the very nature of its duties can have but one allegiance, and that to the whole community.

<u>Resolved</u>: that the Citizens' Committee in all friendliness urge the members of the Boston Police Force and the American Federation of Labor to recognize the reasonableness of this position and ask their co-operation in maintaining it.

5

LETTERS EXCHANGED BETWEEN CHAIRMAN OF COMMITTEE AND JAMES H.VAHEY

August 29, 1919

James J. Storrow, Esq.,
   44 State Street,
      Boston, Mass.

Dear Mr. Storrow:

      Mr. Feeney and I discussed last night with the officers of the Policemen's Union your statement in yesterday afternoon's papers. The men were surprised at your statement and believe that you made it without a full knowledge of all the facts, and they requested me to write you this note.

      Very sincerely yours,

         (Signed) James H. Vahey

August 29, 1919

James H. Vahey, Esq.,
   18 Tremont Street,
      Boston, Mass.

My dear Mr. Vahey:

      Thank you for your letter of this morning.

      I am extremely anxious to see this question from both sides, and it would be a great favor to me if you could arrange for me today a conference with you and Mr. Feeney and the officers of the Policemen's Union. I am anxious to hear the policemen's side of the question.

      Very truly yours,

        (Signed) James J. Storrow

6

LETTER OF CHAIRMAN OF COMMITTEE TO COMMISSIONER CURTIS

Boston, Mass., September 3,1919.

Honorable Edwin U. Curtis,

Police Commissioner, City of Boston,

37 Pemberton Square, Boston,Mass.

My dear Mr. Commissioner:

The Citizens' Committee iis in conference with the offidals of the Police Officers' Union and their counsel in the hope that an amicable and satisfactory solution of the present situation may be found.

We respectfully suggest that we conceive it to be in the public interest while these conferences are still going on that the disciplinary matter now pending before you should remain in statu quo.

Very truly yours,

(Signed) James J. Storrow

7
LETTER OF MAYOR PETERS TO COMMISSIONER CURTIS
September 4, 1919.

Hon. Edwin U. Curtis,
Police Commissioner,
Boston, Mass.

Dear Sir:

I have been watching with keen interest the conferences which have been taking place between the Committee appointed by me a short time ago and the members of
the Boston police force, looking to a solution of the
problems presented by the affiliation of the Police with
the American Federation of Labor, and impressed with the
belief that a solution may be found honorable and satisfactory to the men, and consistent with the principles which
must be observed in an orderly administration of the
Police Force.

With the fullest appreciation of the high responsibility that rests upon you, I must also have in mind the
safety and security of the people. The importance to the
public of having this question settled satisfactorily im-
pels me to ask you to postpone action for a few days only
until developments of the pending conferences may be seen.
If they succeed in solving the problem without requiring you to reach a final decision, friendly discussion
will have achieved a result satisfactory to all concerned.

Very truly yours,

Andrew J. Peters

Mayor

<u>8</u>

REPORT OF EXECUTIVE COMMITTEE TO MAYOR PETERS

Boston, Massachusetts,

Sept. 6, 1919.

Honorable Andrew J. Peters, Mayor,
    City of Boston,
        City Hall, Boston, Mass.

Dear Sir:

      The Citizens' Committee appointed by you to consider the police situation begs to report as follows:

      We recommend the following basis of settlement which we hope will commend itself to Your Honor, the Police Commissioner, and the members of the police force:

(1)   The Boston Policemen's Union should not affiliate or be connected with any labor organization but should retain its independence and maintain its organization for the purpose of assisting its members concerning all questions relating to hours and wages and physical conditions of work.

(2)   That the present wages, hours and working conditions require material adjustment and should be investigated by a committee of three citizens, who shall forthwith be selected by the concurrent action of the Mayor, the Commissioner and the Policemen's Union, and their conclusions communicated to the Mayor and the Police Commissioner, and that thereafter all questions arising relating to hours and wages and physical conditions of work which the Policemen's Union desires to bring before the Commissioner shall be taken up with the Police Commissioner by the duly accredited officers and committees of the Boston Policemen's Union, and should any difference arise relating thereto which cannot be adjusted it shall be submitted to three citizens of Boston selected by agreement between the Mayor, the Police Commissioner

and the Boston Policemen's Union. The
conclusions of the three citizens thus
selected shall be communicated to the
Mayor and the Police Commissioner and
to the Citizens of Boston by publica-
tion. The privisions of this section
shall not apply to any questions of
discipline.

(3)   That nothing should be done to prevent
or discourage any members of the Boston
police force from becoming or continuing to be officers or members of the
Boston Policemen's Union, and that there
should be no discrimination against them
or preferential treatment of them or their
officers because of membership in the
Union.

(4)   That there should be no discrimination on
the part of the members of the Boston Policemen's Union, or any of them, against a
police officer because of his refusal
to join the Boston Policemen's Union or
to continue a member thereof.

(5)   That no member of the Boston Policemen's
Union should be discriminated against be-
cause of any previous affiliation with the
American Federation of Labor.

Respectfully submitted,

EXECUTIVE COMMITTEE

(Signed) James J. Storrow, Chairman
   "   B. Preston, Clark, Secretary
   "   George E. Brock
   "   P. A. O'Connell
   "   James J. Phelan
   "   A. C. Ratshesky
   "   F. S. Snyder

<u>9</u>

Letter of Mayor Peters to Commissioner Curtis
transmitting plan of Citizens' Committee

———————————————————————————————————————

Sept. 6, 1919.

Hon. Edwin U. Curtis,
Police Commissioner,
City of Boston, Mass.

Sir:

I beg to enclose herewith the report of the
Committee of Citizens appointed by me to consider the
police situation. I have examined the report carefully, for I know the patience and thoroughness with
which the Committee has acted, and the extent of time
they have given to a study of the problems.

The report commends itself to me as a wise
method of dealing with the subject, and I recommend it to
your favorable consideration. If acceptable to you
and the men, it affords a speedy, and, it seems to me,
satisfactory settlement of the whole question. You may
rely upon my whole-hearted support in making the plan
suggested in the report effective.

Yours truly,

Andrew J. Peters

Mayor.

10

COMMISSIONER CURTIS'S REPLY TO MAYOR PETERS

CITY OF BOSTON

POLICE DEPARTMENT

OFFICE OF THE COMMISSIONER

September 8, 1919.

Hon. Andrew J. Peters,

    Mayor of the City of Boston.

Dear Sir:

      The Police Commissioner begs to acknowledge receipt of your communication under date of September 6. The Commissioner has given to it that careful consideration which the occasion demands. It will be obvious to Your Honor that the Commissioner cannot consider this communication as having relation to the present duty of the Commissioner to act upon the complaints now pending before him.

      The Commissioner can discover nothing in the communication transmitted by Your Honor and relating to action by him which appears to him to be either consistent with his prescribed legal duties or calculated to aid him in their performance. The Commissioner approves necessary betterment in the economic condition of the Police Force of the City of Boston and has heretofore expressed such approval, but these are not the conditions which require his present action.

      The Commissioner has therefore felt compelled to proceed to make his findings upon the compalints pending before him pursuant to the adjournment of such action heretofore declared.

    I am

            Very respectfully,

              E. U. Curtis

              Police Commissioner
              for the City of Boston

<u>11</u>

Letter of Mayor Peters to Governor Coolidge transmitting plan of Citizens' Committee

September 8, 1919.

Honorable Calvin Coolidge,
Governor of the Commonwealth,
Boston, Mass.

My dear Governor:

Enclosed herewith I am sending to you the correspondence between myself and the Police Commissioner of the City of Boston relative to the police situation.

The solution of the problem presented in the report of my Committee, it seems to me, is a basis for a satisfactory solution of the situation.

I have been and am still trying to get in touch with you on the telephone this afternoon, as I should like to go over the matter with you personally; and I am now sending this information to you at the State House in order that it may be laid before you at the earliest possible moment.

In addition to this correspondence, I personally laid the matter before the Commissioner at a conference this noon and am unable to obtain his approval. I am now presenting it to you with my strong opinion that it offers a basis of solution. I hope you may feel that you can take steps to assist in the solution suggested, and I am glad myself to cooperate in any way possible.

Very truly yours,

Andrew J. Peters

Mayor

12

REPLY OF GOVERNOR COOLIDGE TO MAYOR PETERS

THE COMMONWEALTH OF MASSACHUSETTS
EXECUTIVE DEPARTMENT
BOSTON

September 9,1919.

Hon. Andrew J. Peters,
       Mayor's Office,
             City Hall,Boston.

My dear Mr. Mayor:

Replying to your favor and to the suggestions laid before me by yourself and certain members of your committee, it seems to me that there has arisen a confusion which would be cleared up if each person undertakes to perform the duties imposed upon him by law.

It seems plain that the duty of issuing orders and enforcing their observance lies with the Commissioner of Police and with that no one has any authority to interfere. We must all support the Commissioner in the execution of the laws.

Regarding the matter of improvements in the conditions of employment in the police department of Boston, the law requires that they be initiated by the Mayor and City Council, subject to the approval of the Commissioner. If wages, hours or station houses ought to be improved, such improvements can be initiated by the Mayor and the City Council without any consideration of the making and observance of rules, because over that the Mayor and City Council have no jurisdiction. If justice requires improvements in conditions of employment, I believe such improvements or such parts thereof as can be, should be made forthwith, accompanied by a statement that such additional improvements will be made at the earliest possible time and without reference to any other existing conditions in the police department.

There is no authority in the office of the Governor for interference in the making of orders by the Police Commissioner or in the action of the Mayor and the City Council. The foregoing suggestion is therefore made, as you will understand, in response to a request for suggestions on my part. I am unable to discover any action that I can take.

Yours very truly,

Calvin Coolidge

13

LETTER OF MAYOR PETERS TO GOVERNOR COOLIDGE

September 9, 1919.

Hon. Calvin Coolidge,
Governor of the Commonwealth,
State House, Boston, Mass.

My dear Governor:

Thank you for your letter of September 9.
I had hoped you would consider that the recommendations of the Citizens' Committee pointed the way
towards a practical solution of our problem.

I am sorry that you have not viewed them
in that light and that no counter suggestion has
been presented. Perhaps it is not necessary for me
to add that I am and have been ready to consider the
question of hours, wages and conditions of the police
force. My approval of the Committees plan, which in-
volves taking up such matters forthwith, indicated this.

Very truly yours,

Andrew J. Peters

Mayor

<u>14</u>

S - LP   September 25, 1919

To

   His Honor, The Mayor,

        City Hall, Boston, Mass.

Dear Sir:

        At the conference with your committee held
on Tuesday morning, September 9th, you advised us that at
its termination you were going to interview the Commissioner, and renew the conference with the committee at
a later hour. This you did, and it seems to your chairman
that your interview with the Commissioner forms a necessary part of the records of this entire matter. If, therefore, it is agreeable to you, we would be glad to
incorporate with our report the essence of that conference with the Commissioner.

        We await your judgment and pleasure with
respect to the matter.

                        Very truly yours,

                        (Signed) James J. Storrow

                        Chairman Citizens' Committee

<u>15</u>

CITY OF BOSTON
Office of the Mayor

September 25, 1919.

Mr. James J. Storrow, Chairman,
Citizens' Committee,
44 State St., Boston, Mass.

Dear Mr. Storrow:

I have just received your letter of September 25 in which you request that I outline the essence of my conference with Commissioner Curtis on the morning of Tuesday, September 9, in order that you may incorporate this statement in your report. The facts concerning this conference were as follows:

On September 9 at about one o'clock I visited the Commissioner at his office in Pemberton Square and was assured by him that he had the situation well in hand and had ample means at his disposal for the protection of the city. I asked him whether he did not think he ought to have the State Guard ready for emergencies, and he replied that he did not need it and did not want it.

I then suggested to the Commissioner that the Governor's consideration of the question of protection for the City should then be asked. He replied that it was not necessary, but he consented to see the Governor with me. At the conference in the afternoon with the Governor the same ground was gone over again. The Police Commissioner reiterated his assurances that he had the situation in hand and had made ample provision, and again stated that he did not need or want the State Guard.

Very truly yours,

(Signed) Andrew J. Peters,

Mayor.

<u>16</u>

STATEMENT OF COMMISSIONER CURTIS
<u>Boston Traveler, September 9th</u>

Commissioner Curtis greeted the
announcement of the strike called by the
union policemen with the statement, "I am
ready for anything."

<u>Boston Post, September 9th</u>

In the meantime Commissioner
Curtis, when the news reached him that
the police would probably vote to strike,
said to the Post, "I have no statement
to make as yet." Questioned as to whether
he would still adhere to a previous statement, "I am prepared for all eventualities,"
the commissioner said, "I am ready for anything."

17

Statement of Mayor Peters
Boston Herald, September 10th

Mayor Peters announced last night
that during his conferences with Governor
Coolidge and Police Commissioner Curtis he
had been assured "that measures have been
taken that will afford ample protection to
the people at large."

"Police Commissioner Curtis," he
continued, "assured me that he was in a position to give the people adequate protection.
Governor Coolidge said he was fully prepared
to render support to the police commissioner
in any measures which might be instituted by
the police commissioner. I am relying on
these promises."

<u>18</u>

<u>LETTER OF COMMISSIONER CURTIS TO MAYOR PETERS</u>

September 10, 1919.

To His Honor Andrew J. Peters,
Mayor of the City of Boston.

Sir:

I respectfully submit to Your Honor's consideration that action by Your Honor under provisions of Statute of 1917, Chapter 327, Part I, Section 26, be taken by Your Honor if it shall appear to Your Honor that the present emergency in the City of Boston requires that action. I am of the opinion that tumult, riot or mob is threatened and that the usual police provisions are at present inadequate to preserve order and afford protection to persons and property.

I respectfully suggest that if the facts which I call to Your Honor's attention appear to Your Honor to exist that you will exercise the powers and authority specified and provided by the Statute referred to or by such request as you may deem appropriate to the Commander in Chief for such action as he may deem expedient or necessary.

Respectfully,

(Signed) E. U. Curtis
Police Commissioner for
the City of Boston

19

STATUTE OF 1917, CHAPTER 327, Part I, SECTION 26

Section 26. In case of a tumult, riot, mob or a body of persons acting together by force to violate or resist the laws of the commonwealth, or when such tumult, riot or mob is threatened, or in case of public catastrophe when the usual police provisions are inadequate to preserve order and afford protection to persons and property, and the fact appears to the commander-in-chief, to the sheriff of a county, to the mayor of a city or to the select-men of a town, the commander-in-chief may issue his order, or such sheriff, mayor or selectmen may issue a precept, directed to any commander of a brigade, regiment, naval brigade or battalion, battalion, squadron, corps of cadets or company, within the juris-diction of the officer issuing such order or precept, directing him to order his command, or any part thereof, to appear at a time and place therein specified to aid the civil authority in suppress-ing such violations and supporting the laws; ....

20

STATEMENT OF MAYOR PETERS SEPTEMBER 10th

I have hitherto relied upon the statement of the
Police Commissioner that he had complete control of the situation.

I am now in receipt of a communication from him in
which, in substance, he says that riots are threatened, that
the police provisions are inadequate to preserve order, and
requests me to take the steps contemplated by the statutes
of 1917, Chapter 327, Part 1, Section 26, namely; to call
upon such militia as are within the City of Boston to preserve
order.

This letter, coupled with the occurrences of last
night, when substantial disturbances of public order took
place, shows that the time has come when the business of preserving order should be concentrated in the hands of one person. Under such circumstances, the law places on the Mayor
the power and duty to assume control, and I propose from now
on to see to it that order is preserved and persons and property are protected within the limits of the City of Boston. I
have therefore issued the following proclamation; have called
out such militia as are within the City, and have requested the
Governor of the Commonwealth to furnish me with such additional
tropps as I consider necessary.

. . . .

21

PROCLAMATION OF MAYOR PETERS

September 10, 1919.

It having been made to appear to me, Andrew J.
Peters, Mayor of the City of Boston, that tumult, riot
and violent disturbance of public order have occurred
within the limits of the City of Boston, and the exigency
in my judgment requiring such action, I hereby under the
provisions of Section 6, Chapter 323 of the Acts of 1885,
assume control for the time being of the police of the
said City of Boston, and call upon the Police Commissioner
to execute all orders promulgated by me for the suppression
of such tumult and the restoration of such public order.

Andrew J. Peters
Mayor

22

LETTER OF COMMISSIONER CURTIS TO MAYOR PETERS

September 10, 1919.

To His Honor Andrew J. Peters,

      Mayor of the City of Boston.

Sir:

      Your note of September 10th notifying me that you assume control for the time being of the Police of the City of Boston received. I respectfully await your action.

      Respectfully,

          E. U. Curtis,

                Police Commissioner
                for the City of Boston.

23.

LETTER OF GOVERNOR COOLIDGE TO MAYOR PETERS

September 10, 1919.

Hon. Andrew J. Peters,
Mayor's Office,
City Hall, Boston, Mass.

Dear Mr. Peters:

In accordance with the understanding between
the Police Commissioner and yourself, he has transmitted
to me a copy of his request to you for additional forces
to maintain law and order.

I am awaiting any request you desire to make,
and the Adjutant General is prepared to execute such
request forthwith. I understand that you are in the
process of or have already called to your assistance the
Tenth Regiment of the State Guard. You are at liberty
to call on me for whatever you desire.

Very truly yours,

Calvin Coolidge.

24

LETTER OF MAYOR PETERS TO GOVERNOR COOLIDGE

September 10, 1919.

Hon. Calvin Coolidge,
Governor of the Commonwealth,
Boston, Mass.

Dear Governor:

I have your letter of September
10 and am enclosing herewith a formal request for
additional troops.

Very truly yours,

Andrew J. Peters

Mayor

25

LETTER OF MAYOR PETERS TO GOVERNOR COOLIDGE

September 10, 1919.

Honorable Calvin Coolidge
Governor of the Commonwealth,
Boston, Mass.

Dear Sir:

I have today, acting under the authority given my by Section 6 of Chapter 323 of the Acts of 1885, issued a proclamation assuming control, for the time being, of the police of the City of Boston.

I have also, acting under the authority given me by Section 26 of Part 1 of Chapter 327 of the General Acts of 1917, called out such part of the State Guard as is within the City of Boston to assist in preserving order.

In my judgment this is not adequate for the exigency which ixists. I therefore respectfully request you to order out such a number of troops as you may deem necessary, in addition to those called out by me as above stated. I urgently suggest that the additional number should not be less than three regiments of infantry, fully equipped for field service, to be located as follows:

> One regiment and two battalions at
>   Commonwealth Armory, Boston
>
> One regiment at South Armory, Boston
>
> One battalion at Charlestown Armory

and that the troops which you order out be directed to report at the places specified at five o'clock on Wednesday afternoon, September 10, or as soon thereafter as possible, to Brigadier General John J. Sullivan, who has been called on duty by me.

                    Very truly yours,

                        Andrew J. Peters

                            Mayor

26

STATEMENT OF MAYOR PETERS SEPTEMBER 10, 1919.

I have been so engrossed this morning in arranging the steps necessary to restore and maintain order in the City, that I have only now had opportunity to consider the statement issued a few hours ago by Governor Coolidge, in which he tries to place on me the responsibility for the distressing disturbances which occurred last night. I think I am entitled to state the facts.

Until riot, tumult or disturbance actually takes place, the only person who has authority to police the City is the Police Commissioner and he is appointed by the Governor. The Committee of 34 appointed by me, and myself have made every human effort to avoid the strike of the policemen, but received no co-operation from the Police Commissioner, and no help or practical suggestions from the Governor.

Yesterday, believing that I was entitled to know that provisions had been made for the preservation of law and order in the City in the case of a strike, I consulted with the Police Commissioner. Mr. Curtis said that he had the situation well in hand, had made adequate provisions for any emergency, and assured me there was no occasion for alarm. I asked him whether it would not be wise to have the State Guard mobilized in order that sufficient forces might be on hand in case of an emergency. Police Commissioner Curtis stated in no uncertain terms that he did not wish their aid at that time.

In view of the law which gives to the Police Commissioner the sole right to enforce the law, had I called out the part of the State Guard located in Boston when the Commissioner stated he did not wish their services, I would have had a body of men with no authority, and would have created tremendous confusion. This is so obvious that the statement by the Governor in which he tries to remove the responsibility from Commissioner Curtis and to place it on me is the more astounding.

Furthermore, in a recent communication from the Governor, he states so plainly that no one has any authority to interfere with the Police Commissioner that I should have hesitated to take control of the situation which the Police Commissioner assured me was under control, even had I had the power.

I had no alternative but to give the Police Commissioner a chance to demonstrate that he had adequately provided for the situation. The events of last night having demonstrated that he has misjudged it, I have today been obliged to call out that part of the State Guard situated in Boston and have requested the Governor to issue orders for the mobilization of an additional 3000 men.

27

GOVERNOR COOLIDGE'S PROCLAMATION, Sept. 11, 1919.

The Governor's action in taking charge of the police force was accomplished by the following proclamation:

"The entire state guard of Massachusetts has been called out. Under the constitution the Governor is the commander-in chief thereof by an authority of which he could not, if he chose, divest himself. That command I must and will exercise. Under the law I hereby call upon all the police of Boston who have loyally and in a never-to-be-forgotten way remained on duty to aid me in the performance of my duty in the restoration of order in the city of Boston, and each of such officers is required to act in obedience to such orders as I may hereafter issue or cause to be issued.

"I call on every citizen to aid me in the maintenance of law and order.

                    (Signed) "Calvin Coolidge,
                             "Governor.

"Given at the executive chamber in Boston, this 11th day of September, in the year of our Lord one thousand, nine hundred and nineteen and of the independence of the United States of America the one hundred and forty-third.

"God save the commonwealth of Massachusetts."

<u>28</u>

<u>STATEMENT OF MAYOR PETERS SEPTEMBER 11, 1919</u>

In the situation which now confronts the City of Boston it is of importance that the position of the Executive of the City Government should be made absolutely clear and that every citizen should understand the nature of the issue involved. That issue today is whether the police of the city shall remain an independent force under the sole orders of the representatives of the whole people or whether they should pass under the control of one particular body of its citizens; a body not responsible to the people of Boston.

To this I am just as much opposed as I should be to handing the government over to the bankers, the lawyers, or any other class in the community. I do not mean that any just grievances which the members of the police force may have should not receive fair consideration.

They should, of course, be treated fairly both as to pay and as to hours and conditions of work, but it is unthinkable that such action should be sought or obtained by the police through violation of their oaths of office or refusal to perform their plain duty to the community. The police are the organized force which protects society against crime. Policemen stand on the same basis as members of the Army which protects the community against foreign enemies. For policemen to join an outside organization and strike in order to improve their own private situation is as much a betrayal of the community as it would be for soldiers to strike in order to better their own pay and quarters. In my judgment no compromise on this issue is possible.

I have just received a copy of the proclamation of the Governor of Massachusetts, and his assumption therein of the management of Boston's police force in addition to his powers as commander in chief of the military forces of the Commonwealth.

The Governor having called upon all the citizens to assist him in his efforts, as Mayor of the City, I urge the utmost cooperation of the people of our city in the maintenance of law and order, and pledge my loyal and complete support.

Andrew J. Peters,

Mayor

29

Statement issued by the Boston Chamber of Commerce published in

the papers of August 27th

FAVOR KEEPING POLICE OUT OF UNIONS

Chamber of Commerce admits right to organize, but not

with outside bodies

With reference to the statement published regarding the position of the Boston Chamber of Commerce
in the police controversy, the Board of Directors of the
Chamber has issued the following statement of the
Chamber's attitude in the matter:

"The position of the Boston Chamber of
Commerce in the present police difficulty is as
follows:

"The Chamber represents the business not of
any one class but of the whole community. It looks
at the solution of any community problem solely
from the standpoint of the community and not from
the standpoint of any particular class.

"From that point of view the Chamber is not
in the least antagonistic to organized labor. It
recognizes the rights of all men to organize, and
that the only limitation upon such rights must be
the infringement of the rights of others.

"The present situation with the police, however, is not a question whether the police shall
organize. There is no reason why the police
should not organize within the department or
present any claims or grievances collectively
to the proper authority.

"The sole question is whether their organization should be affiliated with the American
Federation of Labor, and a very brief consideration
of what a policeman really is in the community
shows at once that an organization of police cannot
be associated with an outside body.

"The duty of a policeman is to maintain order in
the community. In other words, a policeman is an of-

29 (Continued)

ficer of the law. In time of trouble between different parties, it is his province to see that the
law is impartially enforced.

"It is therefore manifestly impossible that
he should be actually affiliated with any outside
body which shall in the least influence his action
as an impartial upholder of the law.

"As an illustration, in the event of a sympathetic strike by outside organizations with which
the policemen might be affiliated, the police might be
called upon to strike. In other words, their
allegiance might be divided between the law which
they have sworn to uphold, and an outside organization which they have likewise promised to support.
Such a situation would leave the community without
any protection at all, and is manifestly impossible.

"For this reason it seems to the Chamber that
the present difficulty is not at all with the general principle of organized labor. It is whether
officials of the law should themselves be affiliated
with labor unions and subject to the direction of
their leaders. Looked at in this way it is as impossible for a policeman to be affiliated with labor
unions as for a judge upon the bench. No man can
serve two masters."

<u>30</u>

<u>APPROVAL OF PLAN OF CITIZENS' COMMITTEE BY DIRECTORS</u>

<u>BOSTON CHAMBER OF COMMERCE</u>

September 6, 1919.

Mr. James J. Storrow, Chairman,

      Boston Citizens' Committee,

         44 State Street, Boston, Mass.

My dear Mr. Storrow:

      At a meeting of the Board of Directors held today it was voted that they unanimously approve the recommendations contained in the letter sent to the Mayor by the Executive Committee of your Committee of Thirty-four, and published in this morning's papers; and it was also voted that, if requested by your committee to do so, representatives of the Chamber be authorized to urge the proper state and municipal officers to use their influence to make the recommendations referred to effective.

            Yours respectfully,

            (Signed) James A. McKibben,

                  Secretary.

31

STATEMENT OF BOSTON CHAMBER OF COMMERCE SEPTEMBER 14, 1919

Chamber Hits Reinstatement of Policemen

The Boston Chamber of Commerce issued the following official statement last evening after a special meeting of the directors:

"When the knowledge of the affiliation of the Boston police with the American Federation of Labor became public the Boston Chamber of Commerce immediately placed itself on record as utterly opposed to such affiliation.

"It proffered its services to the public authorities with a view to aiding in the maintenance of public order in the event of a police strike.

"It would have welcomed acceptance of the plan presented by the Mayor's committee and accepted by the Mayor founded upon the principle:

"(1) That the police union disassociate itself from the American Federation of Labor;

"(2) That they effect their own organization which should, fundamentally, have no power to strike;

"(3) That such an organization be aided to present grievances to the authorities and to the public through the medium of a citizens' committee, which should ascertain and report facts and make recommendations upon which public opinion could be formed.

"The Boston Chamber of Commerce is, however, of the opinion that in view of the failure to take such action, and by reason of the fact that the patrolmen deserted their posts of duty, they thereupon placed themselves in a position where the consequences of their deliberate acts must rest upon and follow them.

"In view of the fact that their vote to strike was substantially unanimous the consequence of that act must likewise be universal.

"In the opinion of the Boston Chamber of Commerce there remains nothing for the public authori-

<u>31</u> (Continued)

ties to do save to reconstruct and reorganize the police
force and, as a condition precedent, to deny reinstate-
ment to the men who left their posts of duty.

"We are of the opinion that the authorities
should take such action as may be necessary to assure
proper working conditions and proper remuneration, so
that the Boston police service will attract men of the
highest stamp and in whom the community will have complete confidence.

"Above all, we believe the police force should
be so reorganized that the public may be insured against
the repetition of any abandonment of service upon the
part of officers whose peculiar duty it is to maintain
public order under any and all circumstances."

POLICE IN AMERICA

An Arno Press/New York Times Collection

The American Institute of Law and Criminology.
Journal of the American Institute of Law and Criminology:
Selected Articles. Chicago, 1910–1929.

The Boston Police Strike: Two Reports. Boston, 1919–1920.

Boston Police Debates: Selected Arguments. Boston,
1863–1869.

Chamber of Commerce of the State of New York.
Papers and Proceedings of Committee on the Police Problem,
City of New York. New York, 1905.

Chicago Police Investigations: Three Reports. Illinois,
1898–1912.

Control of the Baltimore Police: Collected Reports.
Baltimore, 1860–1866.

Crime and Law Enforcement in the District of Columbia:
Report and Hearings. Washington, D. C., 1952.

Crime in the District of Columbia: Reports and Hearings.
Washington, D. C., 1935.

Flinn, John J. and John E. Wilkie.
History of the Chicago Police. Chicago, 1887.

Hamilton, Mary E.
The Policewoman. New York, 1924.

Harrison, Leonard Vance.
Police Administration in Boston. Cambridge, Mass., 1934.

International Association of Chiefs of Police.
Police Unions. Washington, D. C., 1944.

The Joint Special Committee.
Reports of the Special Committee Appointed to Investigate
the Official Conduct of the Members of the Board of Police
Commissioners. Boston, 1882.

Justice in Jackson, Mississippi: U.S. Civil Rights
Commission Hearings. Washington, D. C., 1965.

McAdoo, William.
Guarding a Great City. New York, 1906.

Mayo, Katherine.
Justice to All. New York, 1917.

Missouri Joint Committee of the General Assembly.
**Report of the Joint Committee of the General Assembly
Appointed to Investigate the Police Department of the
City of St. Louis.** St. Louis, Missouri, 1868.

National Commission on Law Observance and Enforcement.
Report on the Police. Washington, D. C., 1931.

National Prison Association.
**Proceedings of the Annual Congress of the National Prison
Association of the United States: Selected Articles.**
1874–1902.

New York City Common Council.
**Report of the Special Committee of the New York City
Board of Aldermen on the New York City Police Department.**
New York, 1844.

National Police Convention.
Official Proceedings of the National Prison Convention.
St. Louis, 1871.

Pennsylvania Federation of Labor.
The American Cossack. Washington, D. C., 1915.

Police and the Blacks: U.S. Civil Rights Commission
Hearings. 1960–1966.

Police in New York City: An Investigation. New York,
1912–1931.

The President's Commission on Law Enforcement and
Administration of Justice.
Task Force Report: The Police. Washington, D. C., 1967.

Sellin, Thorsten, editor.
The Police and the Crime Problem. Philadelphia, 1929.

Smith, Bruce, editor.
New Goals in Police Management. Philadelphia, 1954.

Sprogle, Howard O.
The Philadelphia Police, Past and Present. Philadelphia,
1887.

U.S. Committee on Education and Labor.
The Chicago Memorial Day Incident: Hearings and Report.
Washington, D. C., 1937.

U.S. Committee on Education and Labor.
**Documents Relating to Intelligence Bureau or Red Squad of
Los Angeles Police Department.** Washington, D. C., 1940.

U.S. Committee on Education and Labor.
Private Police Systems. Washington, D. C., 1939.

Urban Police: Selected Surveys. 1926–1946.

Women's Suffrage and the Police: Three Senate Documents.
Washington, D. C., 1913.

Woods, Arthur.
Crime Prevention. Princeton, New Jersey, 1918.

Woods, Arthur.
Policeman and Public. New Haven, Conn., 1919.

AMERICAN POLICE SUPPLEMENT

International Association of Chiefs of Police.
**Proceedings of the Annual Conventions of the International
Association of Chiefs of Police.** 1893–1930. 5 vols.

New York State Senate.
**Report and Proceedings of the Senate Committee Appointed
to Investigate the Police Department of the City of
New York.** (Lexow Committee Report). New York, 1895.
6 vols.

THE POLICE IN GREAT BRITAIN

Committee on Police Conditions of Service.
Report of the Committee on Police Conditions of Service.
London, 1949.

Committee on the Police Service.
Minutes of Evidence and Report: England, Wales, Scotland.
London, 1919–1920.

Royal Commission on Police Powers and Procedures.
**Report of the Royal Commission on Police Powers and
Procedure.** London, 1929.

Select Committee on Police.
**Report of Select Committee on Police with the Minutes of
Evidence.** London, 1853.

Royal Commission Upon the Duties of the Metropolitan
Police.
**Minutes of Evidence Taken Before the Royal Commission
Upon the Duties of the Metropolitan Police Together With
Appendices and Index.** London, 1908.

Committee on Police.
**Report from the Select Committee on Police of the
Metropolis.** London, 1828.

DATE DUE
